AMERICAN
WAR LIBRARY

★ ★ ★ ★

★ The Iraq War ★

REBUILDING
IRAQ

Titles in the American War Library series include:

The Iraq War
The Homefront
Life of an American Soldier in Iraq
Rebuilding Iraq
Weapons of War

The American Revolution

The Civil War

The Cold War

The Korean War

The Persian Gulf War

The Vietnam War

The War on Terrorism

World War I

World War II

AMERICAN WAR LIBRARY

★★★★

★ The Iraq War ★

REBUILDING IRAQ

by Debra A. Miller

LUCENT BOOKS

An imprint of Thomson Gale, a part of The Thomson Corporation

THOMSON

GALE

Detroit • New York • San Francisco • San Diego • New Haven, Conn. • Waterville, Maine • London • Munich

© 2005 Thomson Gale, a part of The Thomson Corporation.

Thomson and Star Logo are trademarks and Gale and Lucent Books are registered trademarks used herein under license.

For more information, contact
Lucent Books
27500 Drake Rd.
Farmington Hills, MI 48331-3535
Or you can visit our Internet site at http://www.gale.com

LIBRARY OF CONGRESS CATALOGING-IN-PUBLICATION DATA

Miller, Debra A.
  Rebuilding Iraq / Debra A. Miller.
    p. cm. — (American war library)
  Includes bibliographical references and index.
  ISBN 1-59018-543-9 (hard cover : alk. paper)
  1. Iraq War, 2003—Juvenile literature. 2. Postwar reconstruction—Iraq—Juvenile literature. I. Title. II. Series: American war library.
  DS79.763.M545 2004
  956.7044'31—dc22
                                                          2004010375

Printed in the United States of America

★ Contents ★

Foreword 9

Introduction: "A Long, Hard Slog" 11

Chapter 1: America's Fight with Iraq 15

Chapter 2: Chaos in Postwar Iraq 28

Chapter 3: Growing Terrorism and Resistance 39

Chapter 4: Iraq: An American Responsibility 53

Chapter 5: Creating a New Iraqi Government 63

Chapter 6: Reconstruction Efforts 77

Notes 91

Chronology 95

For Further Reading 98

Works Consulted 99

Index 105

Picture Credits 111

About the Author 112

A Nation Forged by War

The United States, like many nations, was forged and defined by war. Despite Benjamin Franklin's opinion that "There never was a good war or a bad peace," the United States owes its very existence to the War of Independence, one to which Franklin wholeheartedly subscribed. The country forged by war in 1776 was tempered and made stronger by the Civil War in the 1860s.

The Texas Revolution, the Mexican-American War, and the Spanish-American War expanded the country's borders and gave it overseas possessions. These wars made the United States a world power, but this status came with a price, as the nation became a key but reluctant player in both World War I and World War II.

Each successive war further defined the country's role on the world stage. Following World War II, U.S. foreign policy redefined itself to focus on the role of defender, not only of the freedom of its own citizens, but also of the freedom of

people everywhere. During the Cold War that followed World War II until the collapse of the Soviet Union, defending the world meant fighting communism. This goal, manifested in the Korean and Vietnam conflicts, proved elusive, and soured the American public on its achievability. As the United States emerged as the world's sole superpower, American foreign policy has been guided less by national interest and more by protecting international human rights. But as involvement in Somalia and Kosovo prove, this goal has been equally elusive.

As a result, the country's view of itself changed. Bolstered by victories in World Wars I and II, Americans first relished the role of protector. But, as war followed war in a seemingly endless procession, Americans began to doubt their leaders, their motives, and themselves. The Vietnam War especially caused the American public to question the validity of sending its young people to die in places where they were not particularly wanted and for people who did not seem especially grateful.

While the most obvious changes brought about by America's wars have been geopolitical in nature, many other aspects of society have been touched. War often does not bring about change directly, but acts instead like the catalyst in a chemical reaction, accelerating changes already in progress.

Some of these changes have been societal. The role of women in the United States had been slowly changing, but World War II put thousands into the workforce and into uniform. They might have gone back to being housewives after the war, but equality, once experienced, would not be forgotten.

Likewise, wars have accelerated technological change. The necessity for faster airplanes and more destructive bombs led to the development of jet planes and nuclear energy. Artificial fibers developed for parachutes in the 1940s were used in clothing of the 1950s.

Lucent Books' American War Library covers key wars in the development of the nation. Each war is covered in several volumes, to allow for more detail and context, and to provide volumes on often neglected subjects, such as the kamikazes of World War II, or the weapons used in the Civil War. As with all Lucent books, notes, annotated bibliographies, and appendixes such as glossaries give students a launching point for further research. In addition, sidebars and archival photographs enhance the text. Together, each volume in The American War Library will aid students in understanding how America's wars have shaped and changed its politics, economics, and society.

"A Long, Hard Slog"

The attack on Iraq in the spring of 2003 by the United States and its coalition partners resulted in an astonishingly fast, overwhelming military victory. Postwar Iraq, however, posed a series of difficult challenges for U.S. forces, leading many Iraqis and the rest of the world to question whether the U.S. reconstruction process can succeed. These concerns deepened when, pressured by rising costs, increasing troop casualties, and Iraqi protests, U.S. officials began looking for an exit strategy. Whether the United States will stay the course in Iraq long enough to give the country true political and economic stability now is an open question and one that has great impact on the future of Iraq.

A Host of Challenges

The problems and challenges facing the U.S.-led coalition in postwar Iraq loomed large by 2004. They included a crumbling infrastructure and widespread looting and sabotage, both of which hiked reconstruc-tion and military-occupation costs. The United States had also decided to undertake the war without the approval of the United Nations, alienating the international community. This, coupled with America's insistence that it control developments in postwar Iraq, caused many other countries to refrain from sending either troops or reconstruction funds. Yet another serious challenge was a rapidly growing Iraqi insurgency that tried to violently disrupt U.S. attempts to stabilize Iraq. Iraqi rebels mercilessly attacked U.S. troops, U.S. allies, humanitarian agencies, reconstruction workers, and Iraqis who supported the U.S.-led coalition.

Another problem facing America in postwar Iraq was the absence of weapons of mass destruction (WMD). Although finding and destroying WMD was one of President George W. Bush's main justifications for overthrowing Iraqi dictator Saddam Hussein, American troops did not find any such weapons in the year following the war. The absence of WMD threatened to discredit the war effort. Indeed, critics in the American public and in the international community questioned the evidence the Bush administration had relied upon to make its case for war. This caused deep divisions and tension between war supporters and those against the war and challenged many Americans to examine why they went to war and what good it yielded.

Perhaps America's biggest challenge, however, will be finding an honorable way to end the U.S. occupation of Iraq. As the Iraqi insurgency continued, the numbers of U.S. troop casualties increased daily, and the

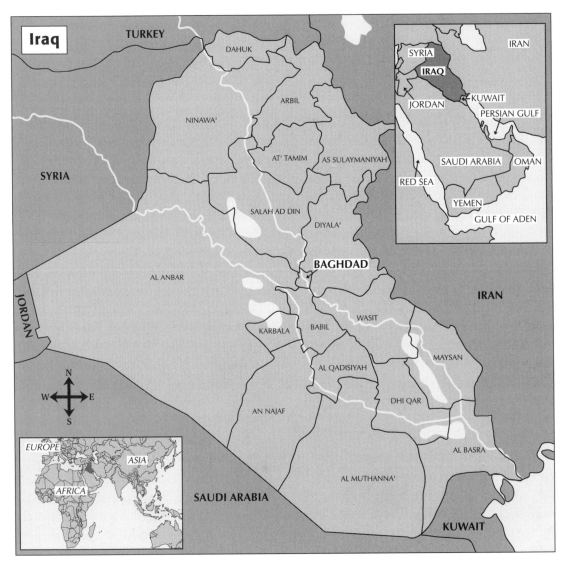

costs to U.S. taxpayers mounted, Americans increasingly questioned whether the war was worth the costs to the United States. Some Americans believed the United States, faced with these challenges, should pull out of Iraq entirely. However, others viewed the occupation as a project that must be seen to conclusion in order to make the undertaking worth the effort. Pulling troops out too early, it was argued, might leave Iraq in such a state of instability and chaos that it could pose a greater threat to the world community than it did under Saddam Hussein. Grappling with when and how to end the U.S. occupation of Iraq, therefore, has become a large question facing America in 2004.

Iraqis themselves have not been overwhelmingly pleased with this undertaking. Although most were grateful for the overthrow of Saddam, they quickly became frustrated with America's inability to make things right. They thought of the United States as a mighty power that surely should be able to turn on the electricity and root out a few insurgents. Many were also dismayed that full sovereignty was not immediately granted to Iraqis. In short, they wanted quick improvements in their lives, to live under self-rule, and to see a rapid removal of U.S. forces.

A Difficult Exit

Faced with these pressures, the United States looked for a way out. U.S. officials planned to reduce troops in the region and sought to speed up the timetable for creating an Iraqi government and Iraqi security forces. These exit strategies, however, proved difficult to implement. Plans to quickly create an interim Iraqi government, for example, were very controversial. Iraq's various ethnic groups—Shias, Sunnis, and Kurds—competed for power. In addition, despite the capture of Saddam in December 2003, insurgent attacks continued, killing both Americans and Iraqis, and threatening the long-term stability of Iraq.

The postwar situation in Iraq, therefore, confronts the United States with a difficult dilemma. On the one hand, there are enormous pressures—political, economic, and military—for the United States to get out of Iraq sooner rather than later. The United States would like nothing better than to hand over power to a friendly Iraqi government, end its occupation of Iraq, and bring U.S. troops home. Such a result would allow the United States to declare victory, both abroad and at home, and cut the enormous drain Iraq is expected to have on the U.S. military and treasury.

On the other hand, if U.S. forces pull out too quickly—before Iraq has developed a stable government and the means to police itself—the country could dissolve into anarchy. For example, insurgents with weapons could stage a coup to try to return pro-Saddam forces to power. Or, a civil war could break out among Iraq's various ethnic groups. Other alienated groups, such as the Kurds, could try to break away from Iraq to form their own country. Such events would leave Iraq in a situation even worse than it was in before the war.

Coalition soldiers are firebombed in the city of Basra. Insurgent attacks are just one of many hazards faced by U.S. personnel in postwar Iraq.

These scenarios might also lead to the establishment of an Iraqi government that is unfriendly to the United States. Indeed, if the Iraqi government that comes to power is anti-American, U.S. interests in the country will be greatly jeopardized. The United States is looking for a partner in the new Iraq; it has vested economic and political interest in the country, and in part, Saddam's overthrow was meant to end over a decade of animosity between the two countries. The United States will thus work hard to ensure that the next Iraqi regime is pro-American, and this will require that it not leave the country prematurely.

Yet remaining in the country is likely to be a long and costly experience for the United States. It requires a continued U.S. military presence to fight Iraqi insurgents, difficult negotiations with Iraq's ethnic groups to find a unifying political solution, and gradual, step-by-step improvements to Iraq's society and economy. Although this type of patient rebuilding will take many years, many more lives, and many more billions of dollars, it may one day give Iraq a chance for political democracy and economic stability. However, for the United States, the road to that bright future, as U.S. secretary of defense Donald H. Rumsfeld wrote in October 2003, will be "a long, hard slog."[1]

Chapter 1

America's Fight with Iraq

raqis lived under the brutal dictatorship of Saddam Hussein for almost three decades. Saddam rose to power in the 1960s as a member of the Baath Party, a political group active in Iraq. The Baath Party first gained power in Iraq in 1963, when it overthrew a military officer who ruled the country. Although the Baath Party itself was quickly overtaken nine months later during another coup, it regained power in 1968. The Baath Party this time was led by a tribe of Sunni Arabs (a minority group of Muslims in Iraq) from the Iraqi town of Tikrit—a tribe that included Saddam. In fact, Saddam's cousin Ahmad Hasan al-Bakr became president of this new government in Iraq. Thanks to this family connection, Saddam soon became an important figure in the Baath Party, second in power only to President al-Bakr.

Saddam's Reign of Terror

The new Baath government was not supported by the people of Iraq. Instead, it relied on repression and terror to stay in power. As author Geoff Simons describes, the Baath Party created "a network of terrorist organizations used to suppress all political opposition."[2] Saddam, who already had a reputation for brutally murdering political foes, was appointed head of the Baath Party's security system.

Over the next several years, Saddam used tactics of terror such as execution, assassination, imprisonment, exile, and torture to get rid of those who might threaten the power of the party. As *New York Times* correspondent and author Elaine Sciolino recounts, "The regime tortured many hundreds of its victims to death in prison . . . ; people were dragged out of their houses and never seen again; in some cases their bodies were thrown in front of their families' houses dreadfully mutilated."[3]

Saddam gradually increased his power and by 1979 had succeeded in seizing the presidency of Iraq from al-Bakr. His first action as president was to purge the Baath

Party of all those who opposed him; in this way he established control over Iraq. At a closed session of the Baath Party's Revolutionary Command Council (the RCC, Iraq's highest body of authority) on July 17, 1979, for example, Saddam slowly and dramatically read the names of those whom he accused as traitors. He then forced remaining members of the council to participate in firing squads to execute the accused. With one blow, he successfully eliminated his enemies and made the remainder his accomplices, leaving no one to challenge his authority.

After gaining power Saddam used terror and torture against anyone who dared criticize or threaten his regime. In 1991 Middle East experts Efraim Karsh and Inari Rautsi described the far-reaching power of Saddam's regime at the time:

> No ordinary Iraqi is immune to the regime's arbitrariness or to the vindic-

Columns of Iraqi soldiers march behind a poster of Saddam Hussein. Saddam ruled Iraq as an absolute dictator from 1979 to 2003.

tiveness of . . . neighbors, friends or even family members. Eavesdropping, spies and informers are a constant threat. A joke or derogatory comments about the President, the RCC, the Baa'th Party or the National Assembly can cost people their lives. . . . They may find themselves detained and tortured without having the slightest clue about the reason for their plight. The luckier detainees may shortly return to their families with no explanation given for their absence; the less fortunate may face long prison terms or even execution.[4]

Indeed, Saddam's regime perfected various methods of torture. His security forces often beat prisoners, twisting their limbs until they broke. Torturers also employed electric shocks and the use of torture machines to remove human limbs such as fingers or even legs. Prisoners were sometimes allowed to freeze and other times were set on fire. Finally, Saddam's forces readily used other physical and psychological torture, such as rape and solitary confinement.

In addition, during Saddam's rule, Iraqi law decreed twenty-four political crimes of treason, all punishable by death. As Middle East expert Con Coughlin has noted, "The definition of these capital offenses was deliberately vague so that any [offense] could be interpreted as treason."[5] For example, one could be given the death penalty for disclosing to an outsider even a very minor piece of information about Iraq. This type of broad definition gave Iraq's security forces virtually unlimited power and forced Iraqis to live in a constant state of fear.

Saddam also completely controlled the army, the media, the court system, the economy, and every government department. Thus, people accused or hurt by his terror system had no recourse. In addition, Iraqis were brainwashed to believe that Saddam was a righteous leader. Freedom of expression was outlawed in Iraq; instead, newspapers, radio, and television were used to glorify Saddam and the Baath Party. Indeed, Saddam deliberately tried to create a cult-like status for himself similar to that of former Soviet dictator Joseph Stalin. Stalin was responsible for a similar state system of institutionalized terror that imprisoned and killed millions of Soviet citizens during the 1930s. Stalin, it has been said, was Saddam's hero.

Saddam Is Armed

Soon after Saddam took power, his regime faced a threat from the neighboring country of Iran. Iran and Iraq had a history of rivalry, but a serious dispute began in 1979. Iran had just undergone a national revolution and declared itself a religious state according to the principles of Shiism, a sect of Islam. Iranian Shias then began stirring up Shias in Iraq, people who had been long persecuted and excluded from political and economic power there. The Ayatollah Khomeini, the leader of the Iranian revolution, openly encouraged Iraqi Shias to rise up against Saddam. For example, Khomeini declared in April 1980, "The people and army of Iraq must turn their backs on the Ba'ath regime and overthrow it."[6] After numerous border skirmishes between the two countries, Iraq attacked Iran on September 22, 1980, leading to an eight-year war.

The United States (along with other nations such as Britain, France, and Russia) did not trust the new fundamentalist Islamic government in Iran. Over the course of the Iran-Iraq War, therefore, these countries provided billions of dollars in military support and surveillance information to Iraq, including materials to help it develop chemical and biological weapons. When the Iran-Iraq War ended in 1988, Iraq was left with a strong military. Indeed, U.S. military support during the Iran-Iraq conflict strengthened the regime of Saddam and turned it into a military power. As investigative journalist Kenneth R. Timmerman explains, "Western businesses and governments helped Iraq assemble one of the most formidable arsenals ever seen in the Middle East. They sold Iraqis tanks, supersonic fighters, chemical weapons, ballistic missiles, and the materials to make an atomic bomb."[7] By the end of the 1980s, Iraq had created the fourth-largest army in the world.

The Persian Gulf War

Saddam soon used his new military power to try to improve Iraq's war-torn economy. After the war, Iraq badly needed income; its oil revenues, however, had significantly dropped. Saddam placed the blame for this financial loss on the neighboring country of Kuwait. Kuwait, Saddam said, was illegally overproducing oil, driving down its price on the world market. When Kuwait failed to cut oil production and take other actions to help Iraq's economy as Saddam demanded, Iraqi troops invaded Kuwait on August 2, 1990, and quickly seized control of the small country.

However, Saddam's invasion of Kuwait turned out to be a huge miscalculation. The United Nations (UN) immediately condemned the action as aggression by one nation against another and demanded that Iraq withdraw its forces. The United Nations first imposed economic sanctions to force Saddam to withdraw. The sanctions prohibited UN member states from buying goods made in Iraq and from selling products to Iraq. When Iraq did not pull out of Kuwait, a massive military attack called Operation Desert Storm was launched by the United Nations on January 16, 1991, and included the United States, many European allies, and also Turkey, Saudi Arabia, and most other Arab nations.

What became known as the Persian Gulf War lasted only a few months and quickly accomplished its stated goals of destroying most of Iraq's military arsenal (including nuclear and chemical facilities) and liberating Kuwait. UN coalition forces, however, refrained from overthrowing Saddam. A British general explained the reasons for this decision, stating, "We did not have a [UN] mandate to invade Iraq or take the country over . . . [and we] would then have found ourselves with the task of trying to run a country shattered by war, which at the best of times is deeply split into factions."[8]

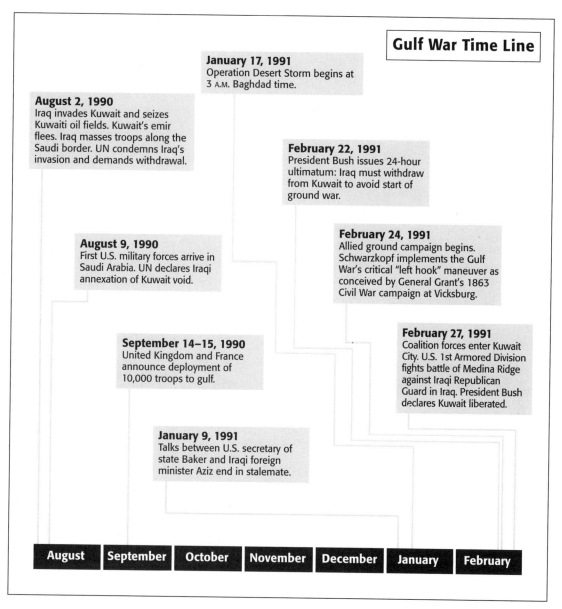

Gulf War Time Line

January 17, 1991
Operation Desert Storm begins at 3 A.M. Baghdad time.

August 2, 1990
Iraq invades Kuwait and seizes Kuwaiti oil fields. Kuwait's emir flees. Iraq masses troops along the Saudi border. UN condemns Iraq's invasion and demands withdrawal.

February 22, 1991
President Bush issues 24-hour ultimatum: Iraq must withdraw from Kuwait to avoid start of ground war.

August 9, 1990
First U.S. military forces arrive in Saudi Arabia. UN declares Iraqi annexation of Kuwait void.

February 24, 1991
Allied ground campaign begins. Schwarzkopf implements the Gulf War's critical "left hook" maneuver as conceived by General Grant's 1863 Civil War campaign at Vicksburg.

September 14–15, 1990
United Kingdom and France announce deployment of 10,000 troops to gulf.

February 27, 1991
Coalition forces enter Kuwait City. U.S. 1st Armored Division fights battle of Medina Ridge against Iraqi Republican Guard in Iraq. President Bush declares Kuwait liberated.

January 9, 1991
Talks between U.S. secretary of state Baker and Iraqi foreign minister Aziz end in stalemate.

| August | September | October | November | December | January | February |

After the war the United Nations voted to keep sanctions in place until all of Iraq's weapons of mass destruction (WMD) programs were fully destroyed. The UN countries believed that Saddam, a dictator who sought greater power and who had already shown his willingness to attack his neighbors, could not be trusted with WMD, especially since Saddam controlled a large amount of the world's oil supplies. They hoped that sanctions would block Saddam from getting items that could be used to build more weapons. A weapons inspection team, called the UN Special Commission on Iraq (UNSCOM), was assembled to monitor the disarming, and in the years that followed, UNSCOM uncovered and destroyed much of Iraq's WMD arsenal.

Saddam, however, often denied weapons inspectors access to Iraq. He lied about the extent or existence of weapons programs and generally obstructed the weapons inspection teams. According to the administration of President George W. Bush, Saddam during this period "repeatedly violated sixteen United Nations Security Council Resolutions designed to ensure that Iraq [did]

not pose a threat."[9] Slowly, Saddam managed to weaken the weapons inspections. For example, in 1997 he declared several sites to be "presidential" and off-limits to inspectors. Saddam later further restricted inspections, accusing the United States of using UNSCOM to spy on Iraq. Because of these and other obstacles, weapons inspections were suspended in 1998.

The sanctions imposed on Iraq ravaged the country. Factories stopped producing goods because they could not acquire foreign-made parts; farmers were unable to import pumps to run their irrigation systems. Similarly, the government lacked material needed to repair Iraq's war-damaged telephone, electricity, road, water, and sewage systems. The sanctions also prevented many necessary

Iraq's Ties to Terror

It remains unclear what link existed between Iraq and terrorism. The Bush administration has taken varying positions on this issue. Shortly after the September 11, 2001 terrorist attacks, for instance, U.S. secretary of state Colin Powell said he could find no clear link between al Qaeda and Saddam Hussein, a position that the Central Intelligence Agency (CIA) maintained for many months.

However, other officials in President Bush's administration believed there was an Iraqi connection to terrorism. Their claims centered around several pieces of evidence. First, it was alleged there was a meeting in Prague, Czech Republic, in April 2001 between the leader of the September 11 hijackers, Mohamed Atta, and an Iraqi intelligence agent. After an investigation, however, the Czechs concluded that the report could not be substantiated.

Other U.S. officials claimed that an al Qaeda terrorist camp had been established in northern Iraq. This camp was allegedly providing a haven for a terrorist known as Abu Musab al-Zarqawi, a senior al Qaeda leader who had reportedly escaped from Afghanistan into Iraq. The Bush administration reasoned that Saddam's secret police most certainly knew of al-Zarqawi's presence, thus establishing that Iraq was harboring terrorists. President Bush made this claim in an October 7, 2002, speech to the nation.

In addition, in October 2002 CIA director George J. Tenet claimed that there was credible evidence suggesting that al Qaeda had sought contacts in Iraq that could help them acquire weapons of mass destruction. Tenet also stated that Iraq had provided training to al Qaeda members. However, because none of these pieces of evidence has ever been fully proven, there remains a wide variety of opinion on whether Saddam's regime had ties to terrorism.

goods from reaching ordinary Iraqi citizens. For example, the sanctions barred items such as medical supplies, school books, building supplies, materials needed to provide drinkable water and sanitation, and items needed for industry and oil production. Iraqis no longer had access to recreational items such as computers, chess boards, magazines, bicycles, and cameras.

As a result, the sanctions were increasingly criticized as inhumane. Many critics said they caused unjustified suffering for the Iraqi people without hurting Saddam. Indeed, over the years sanctions impoverished the Iraqi people, created severe health and food crises, and by limiting food and medicine, caused the deaths of as many as five hundred thousand Iraqi children. Although the sanctions added to the devastation in Iraq, they have been credited with limiting to some degree Saddam's ability to import items that could be used to produce weapons.

The United Nations tried to help the Iraqi people by creating an oil-for-food program under which Iraq was allowed to sell oil to purchase food, medicine, and other necessities. The program helped a little but in many cases Saddam refused to purchase humanitarian items for his people. He instead sold oil illegally and used the money to build new palaces for himself and to provide luxuries for supporters of his regime. In this way, Iraqis continued to suffer under his rule.

In the years following the Persian Gulf War, many countries abandoned the issue of Iraq. The United States and Britain, however, maintained a military presence there and re-peatedly conducted air and missile strikes on Iraqi targets throughout the 1990s. These military efforts sought to restrict Iraqi military movements and aggression. For example, in Operation Desert Strike in 1996, strikes were made to stop Saddam from persecuting the Kurds, an Iraqi ethnic group. Similarly, in Operation Desert Fox in 1998, air strikes were made as a result of Saddam's defiance of weapons inspections. The United States was criticized by other countries for these efforts because, unlike the UN-authorized Persian Gulf War of 1991, the United States conducted these later military strikes on its own initiative and without UN approval.

At the end of the decade, despite the international efforts to disarm Iraq and the hardships endured by the Iraqi people, Saddam remained defiant. His regime had survived, he was no longer subject to weapons inspections, and many wondered if he was somehow finding ways to rebuild his military arsenal.

The Axis of Evil and the U.S. Push for War

The September 11, 2001, terrorist attacks by the group al Qaeda renewed America's determination to disarm Saddam. Shortly after the attack, President Bush declared a war on terrorism, promising to use every resource and tool, even war, to disrupt and defeat the global terror network. In 2002 Bush warned of another facet of terrorism—an "axis of evil" consisting of three countries: Iraq, Iran, and North Korea. He charged that these states sponsored terrorism and sought to develop chemical, biological, and nuclear weapons:

> States like these, and their terrorist allies, constitute an axis of evil, arming to threaten the peace of the world. By seeking weapons of mass destruction, these regimes pose a grave and growing danger. They could provide these arms to terrorists, giving them the means to match their hatred. They could attack our allies or attempt to blackmail the United States. In any of these cases, the price of indifference would be catastrophic. [10]

Bush said Iraq, in particular, was a nation that was hiding something from the rest of the world. The president claimed, for example, that the Iraqi regime had plotted to develop anthrax, nerve gas, and nuclear weapons for over a decade and had already used chemical weapons to murder thousands of its own citizens. Bush hinted that military action might be used by the United States in the near future, stating, "The United States of America will not permit the world's most dangerous regimes to threaten us with the world's most destructive weapons." [11]

Soon after the speech, America's intentions to attack Iraq became clear. Officials from the Bush administration began openly threatening war and advocating removing Saddam from power. In a speech given on August 26, 2002, for example, Vice President Dick Cheney warned:

Wearing hazardous materials suits, UN weapons inspectors search for evidence of weapons of mass destruction in Iraq in 2002.

Armed with an arsenal of these weapons of terror, and seated atop ten percent of the world's oil reserves, Saddam could then be expected to seek domination of the entire Middle East, take control of a great portion of the world's energy supplies, directly threaten America's friends throughout the region, and subject the United States or any other nation to nuclear blackmail.[12]

Opposition to the War Plan

The U.S. plan for military action against Iraq, however, faced widespread criticism, both at home and abroad. Indeed, the suggestion of war sparked some of the largest antiwar demonstrations in history, not only in the United States but also in countries around the world. In addition, many of America's European and Arab allies denounced the idea of war. For example, important members of the UN Security Council (the group of UN members who have the right to reject proposed UN actions), such as Russia, Germany, and France, opposed a U.S. invasion of Iraq and pushed for a diplomatic solution. Only Tony Blair, the prime minister of Britain, stood squarely behind the United States.

Many opponents of a war in Iraq charged that there was no link between Iraq and the al Qaeda terrorists who had attacked the United States on September 11, 2001. Indeed, some argued that a war against Iraq could actually weaken the war on terrorism because it could divert resources away from the hunt for terrorists. Still others worried that there was no plan to stabilize Iraq after Saddam was removed from power. Also, the cost of war and postwar reconstruction, they said, would be too high for the United States to assume alone.

Perhaps the most frequent claim, however, was that UN weapons inspections had worked and that there was little evidence that Saddam still possessed nuclear or missile capabilities. Critics charged that war, therefore, was not justified because Iraq did not pose an imminent threat to the United States or other nations. The fact that Iraq has the second-largest oil reserves in the world also raised the eyebrows of those wary of war. They charged that the push for war with Iraq was not really about countering a threat from WMD; instead, they claimed, the real goal was to remove Saddam from power and install a pro-American government in Iraq in order to secure U.S. access to Iraqi oil.

Controversy also surrounded the strategy of the war plan; going to war against Iraq would be part of a new policy known as preemption. This was a strategy the Bush administration introduced to take action against countries that do not pose an immediate threat but may, at some time in the future, endanger U.S. interests. The idea of preemptive action was controversial in America. Proponents of preemption argued that after September 11, 2001, the United States could not afford to sit back and be attacked first. Opponents of preemption, however, argued that attacking a nation without certain cause put the United States in the position of being an aggressor and also ran the risk of judging a nation's intentions incorrectly. Furthermore, it was warned that preemptive action might encourage other countries to adopt aggressive policies. Such a scenario would increase the amount of violence in the world, not reduce it. Such debates about the reasons for going to war and how it should be approached continued through 2002.

Diplomatic Efforts to Disarm Iraq

President Bush at first agreed to work with the United Nations to contain the Iraqi threat. On September 12, 2002, in a widely publicized address to the United Nations, Bush set forth his case against Saddam, citing Iraq's failure to disarm as required by numerous UN resolutions. He also raised questions about the period since UN inspectors were last allowed into Iraq. He concluded, "We know that Saddam Hussein pursued weapons of mass murder even when inspectors were in the country. Are we to assume that he stopped when they left? The history, the logic and the facts lead to one conclusion. Saddam's regime is a grave and gathering danger."[13] The president demanded that Iraq disarm, and he urged the United Nations to renew weapons inspections, which it did on November 8, 2002, when Resolution 1441 was approved by a unanimous vote. The resolution set up a new weapons inspections process and warned Iraq that it would "face serious consequences"[14] if it failed to comply. Iraq agreed to allow weapons inspectors back into Iraq, and inspections by the International Atomic Energy Agency (IAEA) and the newly formed UN weapons inspection team, called the UN Monitoring, Verification, and Inspection Commission (UNMOVIC), began in late November 2002.

IAEA and UNMOVIC inspections over the next several months did not discover any weapons of mass destruction. Despite this result, the United States concluded that Saddam had failed to cooperate and had hid evidence, thus violating UN resolutions. On February 24, 2003, the United States, Britain, and Spain circulated a second UN resolution to authorize war against Iraq; the proposed resolution stated that "Iraq has failed to take the final opportunity afforded to it."[15]

However, key members of the UN Security Council, particularly France, Germany, and Russia, refused to authorize military action. These countries did not think Iraq posed an immediate threat. They believed that continued inspections would best contain Saddam. When it became clear that the United States could not muster UN support for war, President Bush decided to invade Iraq and remove Saddam from power on his own initiative, as the leader of a group of nations that he called "a coalition of the willing." This coalition included some thirty nations that agreed to back the U.S. war action. However, most countries were partners in name only; Britain and Australia were the only ones that provided any significant military assistance.

In a speech to the nation on March 17, 2003, Bush announced the U.S. war plans, stating:

Today, no nation can possibly claim that Iraq has disarmed, and it will not disarm so long as Saddam holds power. . . . All the decades of deceit and cruelty have now reached an end. Saddam and his sons must leave Iraq within 48 hours.

Protests Against the War in Iraq

The plan to attack Iraq inspired some of the largest peace demonstrations in history. All over the world, in European, Asian, South American, and Arab countries, hundreds of peace rallies were held to denounce the rush to war. Large antiwar protests also sprang up in the United States.

Over the weekend of February 15, 2003, for example, it was estimated that as many as 15 million people demonstrated around the globe. Protesters that weekend in Britain were estimated at 2 million; in Spain, 2 million; in Italy, 1 million; in Germany, 0.5 million; and in France, 0.3 million. In New York City alone, crowds numbered more than 375,000, and many Americans protested in other cities and small towns. Thousands more attended demonstrations in other countries, such as Ireland, Greece, Russia, and Turkey. After the invasion of Iraq, another round of demonstrations erupted, bringing as many as 5 million people to the streets around the world. Many said the protests made clear that the people of the world did not want a war in Iraq. Others, however, dismissed the demonstrations as the politics of a small fringe of society. In any case, the protests were ultimately unable to stop or delay the U.S. invasion of Iraq.

Antiwar protesters clash with police in San Francisco. Although protests were held around the world, the invasion of Iraq continued as planned.

Their refusal to do so will result in military conflict, commenced at a time of our choosing.[16]

When Saddam did not leave Iraq as demanded by the United States, U.S. troops invaded.

The 2003 U.S. Military Victory

The American attack on Iraq began with a surprise missile strike on the evening of March 19, 2003, targeting a site in Baghdad believed to be the command post for Saddam and top leaders of his regime. The United States hoped, in one decisive blow, to kill Saddam and destroy his regime. However, the mission failed and Saddam and his supporters escaped, as later video- and audiotapes revealed.

Next, on March 21, 2003, the U.S. military began an all-out air and land assault on Iraq, a campaign the military called Op-

U.S. air strikes level Baghdad's city center in March 2003. As the strikes continued, ground troops began marching toward Iraq's capital.

eration Iraqi Freedom. The first round of air strikes dropped more than thirteen hundred cruise missiles and bombs on Iraqi targets in Baghdad. Targets included headquarters and facilities used by the Republican Guard, Saddam's most elite troops. The air campaign continued unabated in the following days, pounding Baghdad day and night, taking out government facilities, destroying Iraq's air defenses, and hitting Republican Guard positions.

Meanwhile, U.S. and British forces numbering about 150,000 troops began a long march toward Baghdad. The land assault got off to a highly successful start, raising expectations among the U.S. public that the war could be won quickly and painlessly. However, coalition ground forces quickly met fierce resistance from Iraqi fighters in the southern cities of Basra and Nasiriya. Also, the column of American tanks headed for Baghdad was repeatedly attacked by small bands of Iraqi guerrilla fighters known as the Saddam Fedayeen, or "Martyrs of Saddam," who were heavily armed. On top of these troubles, the U.S. move toward Baghdad was slowed by the weather. A huge sandstorm disrupted the American convoys, blinded night-vision goggles, and damaged equipment, including guns, helicopters, and computers.

Despite the problems, U.S. and British troops made steady progress. Iraqi oil fields were quickly secured, and the U.S. antimissile system shot down most Iraqi missiles launched into Kuwait, preventing any damage to U.S. command centers there. Most importantly, American forces traveled deep into Iraq to the capital of Baghdad. There, U.S. forces destroyed Republican Guard units that were expected to put up a much tougher fight.

Finally, on April 9, the world watched as Iraqi citizens and U.S. marines toppled a towering bronze statue of Saddam in the center of Baghdad. As the statue came crashing to the ground, a crowd of jubilant Iraqis cheered loudly, danced for joy, and hit the statue with their shoes, a gesture of contempt in Iraq. At this moment, symbolically at least, the regime of Saddam collapsed. A short time later, on May 2, 2003, just forty-five days after the war began, President Bush proudly stood on the flight deck of the aircraft carrier USS *Abraham Lincoln,* in front of a banner that read "Mission Accomplished," and declared that "major combat operations in Iraq [had] ended."[17]

Chapter 2

Chaos in Postwar Iraq

Although the war appeared to be a great military success, the sudden overthrow of Saddam left the country in a state of utter chaos. The United States slowly began the massive effort to restore order, restart essential services, and begin rebuilding Iraq. But it soon became clear that the U.S. postwar plans were not adequate for the job. U.S. forces lacked the manpower that was required to keep the peace in the delicate postwar environment. They also were not prepared to deal with the sheer need of the country; basic necessities such as clean water and food were insufficient, and many people panicked, which led to chaos. The United States was criticized for not anticipating that this would be the situation after the war. The war effort endured further scrutiny when it failed to immediately capture Saddam or uncover weapons of mass destruction, the main justification for the war.

Death and Disaster

The war took a large toll on the Iraqi population. They had to cope with death, total dis-

ruption of normal life, and humanitarian disasters. During the war American forces consciously tried to select targets in a way that would limit "collateral damage," the military's term for civilian deaths. Nevertheless, according to a survey by the Associated Press, "at least 3,240 civilians died . . . between March 20, when the war began, and April 20, when the fighting was dying down."[18] Thousands more civilians were injured by the attacks. And although U.S. military officials touted the low casualty rate for U.S. soldiers—a total of 138 American soldiers were killed during the war—unmentioned in the U.S. reports were the unknown thousands of Iraqi troops who were killed and wounded in the fighting.

Essential services such as water, food, and electricity were abruptly cut off during the war. Even before the war, however, Iraq's basic services were in disarray as a result of the Iran-Iraq War, the Persian Gulf War, the corruption of the Saddam regime, and twelve years of UN-imposed economic sanctions. For example, as many as 16 million Iraqis, or the majority of the population, depended entirely on food shipped into Iraq as part of the UN's oil-for-food program (OFFP). Iraq's electrical grid and other public works were in similar disrepair from years of neglect and underfunding.

Another war exacerbated these problems. There was an immediate shortage of food since the war disrupted food shipments from outside Iraq. In addition, the fighting knocked out electrical power for water treatment plants, destroying the only source of safe drinking water and forcing people to drink water from sources that may have been contaminated by sewage or other pollutants.

On May 12, 2003, the World Health Organization (WHO) warned that parts of Iraq could experience an epidemic of cholera, a disease caused by germs from fecal contamination of water supplies that results in severe sickness and sometimes death.

Health care was also largely unavailable. The fighting and postwar looting damaged many hospitals and health facilities just when Iraqis injured in the violence most needed medical care. Also, during and after the war

An Iraqi civilian receives medical care after the March 2003 air strikes. Thousands of Iraqi civilians were killed in the first month of the war.

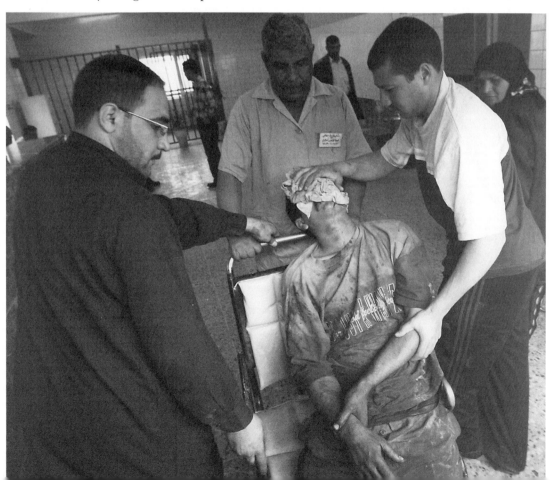

many health facilities lost electrical power. As law and order disappeared with the fall of the regime, medical staff often failed to report to work because of fears for their safety. Although Baghdad hospitals coped initially, by April 11 the Red Cross claimed that even "the medical system in Baghdad [had] virtually collapsed"[19] because of war damage and looting.

By the end of the war, daily life in Iraq had become a nightmare. Student writer Homayra Ziad reported on conditions that existed in postwar Iraq as of May 2003:

With the temperature hovering at 110 degrees, there are only four hours of electricity—two in the morning and two in the evening—available daily in Baghdad. Due to contaminated water supplies, water is limited. Cooking gas is unavailable, and lines for gasoline snake through the city from 5 A.M. onward, with wait-times of up to 12 hours. . . . There is limited food as—again, due to security concerns—few stores remain open. Food supplies largely come from neighboring countries . . . and are distributed through mosques. . . . The state of hospitals is pitiful. . . . The plundering has been so thorough . . . that "patients were [lifted] off as their beds were looted." Most hospitals are running out of medicine.[20]

Temporary Relief

Fortunately for Iraqis, the world responded quickly to their plight. After the war the United Nations resumed distribution of OFFP food for six months and earmarked almost $13 billion to pay for additional food, medicine, and industrial goods. Also, the UN World Food Program (WFP), the world's largest humanitarian agency, distributed 200,000 tons of food to Iraqis during the first few weeks following the war—enough to feed 14 million people (or half of the Iraqi population) for one month. On June 1, 2003, it began sending 480,000 tons of food each month to feed all 27 million Iraqis. In addition, on May 20, 2003, the WHO began bringing basic health services in Iraq back to their prewar levels, an effort that it estimated would cost up to $180 million. The United States, Britain, Spain, and Italy quickly pledged to support this program.

By July 15, 2003, at least thirty-six countries had pledged or contributed funds to support the humanitarian effort in Iraq, including the United States, Britain, Canada, Japan, Australia, Germany, Norway, Denmark, the United Arab Emirates, Saudi Arabia, Spain, and Kuwait, to name a few. In addition, the European Union, a coalition of fifteen European nations, donated approximately $852 million in humanitarian aid.

As a result of these efforts, Iraq did not suffer from a food shortage. Basic health care services also were largely resumed fairly quickly. However, restoration of other basic services, such as water, electricity, and communications, was slow, hampered by looting and continuing sabotage. During the summer of 2003 these hardships in postwar Iraq proved difficult for long-suffering Iraqis who had hoped that American know-how and technology could quickly improve their damaged country.

Looting and Insecurity

One of the most discouraging developments in postwar Iraq was an unprecedented wave of crime and looting. The quick removal of Saddam's regime left a huge power vacuum, resulting in chaotic security conditions. Iraqis who suffered under Saddam's regime sought revenge by destroying government sites. Poor Iraqis saw a chance to steal items they desperately needed or could sell for cash. Also, criminals let loose from Iraqi jails just before the war began preying on law-abiding Iraqis. As one Iraqi, Mahmoud Ahmed Uthman, describes it, "We used to have a brutal dictatorship that controlled everything. . . . When the government collapsed, there was nothing left except a great emptiness. And that emptiness has been filled with chaos."[21]

The looting destroyed government buildings, hospitals, museums, universities, banks, businesses, and power and water facilities, gutting them of virtually anything and everything that could be carried off. For example, precious antiquities were stolen from Iraqi museums and archaeological sites, critical medical supplies were looted from hospitals, and essential parts were removed from utility facilities. The initial looting soon turned into a chronic crime wave: Armed bands patrolled highways, hijacking private cars and trucks carrying humanitarian supplies, and criminals mugged citizens and burglarized their homes.

Museum Relics Returned

One of the worst cases of looting in postwar Iraq was the theft of precious heirlooms and artifacts from Iraq's National Museum in Baghdad. This museum housed some of the world's oldest treasures. Archaeologists claimed that major, irreplaceable treasures were stolen, including items such as a lyre from the ancient Sumerian city of Ur that was estimated to be over four thousand years old. Initially, it was believed that thousands of other such artifacts had been stolen, too.

Fortunately, by the end of 2003 many of the missing items had been recovered. Of the 170,000 items that were thought to have been taken, only about 3,000 items remained missing. Indeed, hundreds of artifacts and thousands of ancient manuscripts had been stored in underground vaults to protect them from the war's damage. For example, the treasures of Nimrud (an ancient Assyrian city), which date to about 900 B.C., were located in good condition in a secret vault in Iraq's Central Bank. Other artifacts, which had in fact been stolen by looters, have since been discovered in houses and fields throughout Iraq.

The looting and instability slowed the provision of humanitarian aid and delayed efforts to get Iraq's electricity and other utilities up and running after the war. The delays in restoring electricity and telecommunications, in turn, kept businesses and banks closed, and with armed robbers on the highway, trade and commerce virtually stopped. In addition, the destruction caused by the looting added to the war's damage, vastly increasing reconstruction costs.

A Lack of Planning

The deteriorating security conditions in postwar Iraq graphically revealed the inadequacy of U.S. plans for how to stabilize the country after Saddam's regime fell. The Bush administration was criticized for not properly anticipating the need for security in postwar Iraq and for underestimating the amount of work it would take to rebuild the country. Shortly after the war Republican senator Richard G. Lugar stated in a Senate Foreign

Relations Committee meeting, "I am concerned that the administration's initial stabilization and reconstruction efforts have been inadequate. . . . The planning for peace

A U.S. soldier stands guard over an Iraqi looter. After Saddam's government was toppled, looting took place throughout Iraq on a large scale.

was much less developed than the planning for war." Meanwhile, Democratic senator Joseph R. Biden Jr. complained, "When is the president going to tell the American people that we're likely to be in the country of Iraq for three, four, five, six, eight, 10 years, with thousands of forces and spending billions of dollars?"[22]

Indeed, it is clear in hindsight that U.S. leaders miscalculated the difficulty of occupying and rebuilding Iraq. Many American expectations envisioned grateful Iraqis cheering the U.S. soldiers as "liberators" and a relatively easy road to democracy and rebuilding. As Senator Biden put it, the Bush administration "believed [Americans] would find an oil-rich, functioning country, that we'd be met by cheering crowds, that all we had to do was sweep out the top Baathist layers, implant our favorite [Iraqi] exiles and watch democracy take root as the bulk of the [U.S.] troops returned home by Christmas."[23]

Indeed, one of the most striking examples of prewar wishful thinking was a plan to use Iraqi police and soldiers to retain order. Contrary to American expectations, however, both police officers and Iraqi soldiers disappeared when the war started. The U.S. military, therefore, was left as the only peacekeeping force in Iraq. On top of this, because the war plans had called for a lean fighting force, not enough American soldiers were in Iraq at the end of the war to maintain order. At the end of the war only about twenty thousand American troops were stationed in Baghdad, a city of about 4.5 million people. These troops had other important respon-

sibilities that prevented them from patrolling for looters; they were not trained or equipped to undertake day-to-day policing responsibilities. In addition, the U.S. government initially downplayed the security problem and avoided using force against looters; U.S. officials feared that the image of American soldiers firing at Iraqis would antagonize the Arab world, which was already opposed to the U.S. attack on Iraq.

As looting escalated, however, military officials realized something had to change. In April 2003 U.S. troops began joint patrols with Iraqis, including several hundred Iraqi police officers who reported to duty without pay. Also, the United States replaced Jay Garner, an American army general charged with overseeing reconstruction, with a civilian administrator, L. Paul Bremer III. His appointment marked a turning point in the postwar administration of Iraq. Bremer vowed to restore order to the chaotic country. In an effort to demonstrate U.S. resolve, he immediately arrested about three hundred violent criminals who had been released by Saddam. As part of the tough new security policy, Bremer authorized U.S. military forces to shoot looters. He also increased patrols, banned assault weapons, hired more police officers, and began trying to rid the country of Baath Party supporters.

Despite these efforts, months after U.S. troops first entered Baghdad, America was still trying to secure Iraq. Ironically, congressional investigations in October 2003 revealed that, prior to the war, the U.S. State Department had actually predicted many of the problems that arose in postwar Iraq. In April 2002 a State Department study titled the "Future of Iraq Project" gathered more than two hundred Iraqi lawyers, engineers, businesspeople, and other experts into groups to study various problems that would likely arise in Iraq.

The study predicted that Iraq's electrical and water systems were severely dilapidated and would need much repair work. The study also said that Iraqi society was so brutalized by Saddam's rule that many Iraqis might react coolly to American rebuilding efforts. Most telling, the study predicted there would be widespread looting after the fall of Saddam's government, caused in part by thousands of criminals set free from prison, and it recommended the immediate use of force to prevent the chaos. The study urged U.S. officials to "organize military patrols by coalition forces in all major cities to prevent lawlessness, especially against vital utilities and key government facilities."[24]

The findings of the study, however, were not taken into account by U.S. military planners. As criticism of the military's postwar plans continued, Bush appointed national security adviser and close presidential aide, Condoleezza Rice, as head of the Iraq Stabilization Group. Meanwhile, the violence in Iraq continued to escalate.

The Missing Weapons of Mass Destruction

Another significant problem that emerged during the chaos of postwar Iraq involved finding Iraq's weapons of mass destruction (WMD). To the surprise of U.S. military planners, Iraqi troops did not use chemical or other WMD during the war. Although American soldiers fighting in Iraq found indicators of chemical weapons, such as gas masks, protective suits, nerve gas antidotes, and training manuals, the weapons themselves were not found in the areas known to have been occupied by Iraqi soldiers.

When the war ended, in addition to its other responsibilities, the U.S. military was asked to search for Iraq's supposedly hidden stocks of WMD. Many thought they would not be difficult to find: It was expected that troops would quickly stumble upon illegal weapons left behind by Iraq's government and military forces. However, initial coalition efforts to search for such weapons proved unfruitful.

Since the presence of such weapons in Iraq was President Bush's main justification for going to war, their absence at war's end placed the Bush administration under heavy domestic and international scrutiny. Critics accused the administration of intentionally misleading the public by overstating the weapons threat posed by Saddam in order to gain support for the war. An editorial in the *New York Times,* for example, read, "With every passing day, American credibility is called into question. . . . The chief justification for invading Iraq was to get rid of Baghdad's stores of chemical and biological agents and dismantle its effort to produce a nuclear bomb."[25]

Initially, President Bush steadfastly insisted that the hidden weapons would be found, cautioning that it would just take time. The United States intensified the search and put David Kay, a respected former international weapons inspector and envoy from the U.S. Central Intelligence Agency (CIA), in charge of a U.S. task force searching for weapons in Iraq. Bush also ordered the CIA to determine whether it may

Because the presence of weapons of mass destruction in Iraq was President Bush's justification for declaring war, he faced sharp criticism when none were found.

have erred in its prewar assessments of Iraq's weapons programs.

U.S. officials eventually began to suggest that WMD stockpiles might never be found because they might have been destroyed before the war. One source, an Iraqi military intelligence officer who claimed that he oversaw part of Iraq's chemical weapons program, appeared to support this view. The officer claimed that, beginning in the mid-1990s, Iraq had destroyed some stockpiles of unconventional weapons, sent some to Syria, and recently had burned some warehouses of chemical agents. The officer also said that Iraq destroyed chemical weapons and biological warfare equipment a few days before the war began.

This informant further explained that, instead of maintaining WMD stockpiles, Saddam focused on preserving the ingredients for future development of such weapons so that he could restart WMD programs once inspectors were gone. This way, he could work on weapons projects that would be almost impossible for weapons inspectors to detect— for example, production of chemical ingredients that were not prohibited as weapons but that could be quickly made into chemical weapons. These claims were confirmed by other Iraqi officials in U.S. detention.

Finally, in an interim report to Congress in early October 2003, Kay confirmed that his team had not yet found stocks of illicit weapons—no chemical or biological agents, no signs that Iraq was working on a nuclear program, and no evidence of an attempt to buy uranium from Africa, as had been claimed in Bush's 2003 State of the Union address. A few months later Kay resigned, saying he had concluded that Iraq did not have a nuclear program or any large stockpiles of chemical or biological weapons.

Saddam Survives to Rally Resistance

Adding to the chaos, confusion, and fear in postwar Iraq was the realization that Saddam had survived the initial missile strike at the start of hostilities. Removing Saddam was considered essential to allay the fears of still-frightened Iraqis who had been traumatized by his brutal regime for decades and who worried that he might try to return to power.

The U.S. military, therefore, acting on tips and intelligence information, made repeated attempts to attack locations where Saddam and other members of the Iraqi leadership were thought to be meeting. On April 7, for instance American bombers dropped four huge bombs on a compound in Baghdad where Saddam was believed to be meeting with his sons and top leaders. However, two days after the bombing, dozens of Iraqis reported seeing Saddam alive. U.S. forces therefore continued to target Saddam. On April 10 they attacked and later bombed a mosque in Baghdad where Saddam was spotted, but still did not kill the Iraqi leader. On April 30 a letter appeared in a London-based Arabic newspaper in which Saddam urged Iraqis to rebel against America, calling the United States the "infidel, criminal, murderous and cowardly occupier." He also promised that those who collaborated with the Americans would be punished, and predicted that "the day of liberation and victory will come." [26] The letter confirmed Iraqis' worst fears—Saddam was still alive and planning a comeback.

Refusing to give up its search, the U.S. military announced rewards for the most-wanted Iraqi leaders and issued to troops a deck of fifty-five playing cards, each showing the picture and name of an Iraqi leader. The cards were meant to familiarize soldiers with their targets and aid their capture of Saddam and his top aides. By Fall 2003, most of these leaders had been killed or taken into custody by U.S. forces, including notables such as Ali Hassan al-Majid, known as "Chemical Ali" for ordering a chemical attack that killed thousands of Kurds in 1988. Tariq Aziz, Iraq's deputy prime minister and public spokesman for the regime, was also captured, as was General Abid Hamid Mahmoud al-Tikriti, Saddam's top aide. In July even Saddam's two sons, Uday and Qusay, were located; they were killed in a gunfight with U.S. troops. Saddam, however, remained at large—despite a $25-million bounty offered by the United States for information leading to his capture or providing evidence of his death.

Communications from Saddam continued as months passed; in each, Saddam urged Iraqis to resist U.S. forces. For example, an audiotape broadcast by the Arabic television station Al Jazeera on July 4, 2003, warned that "the coming days will, God willing, be days of hardship and trouble for the infidel invaders."[27] Yet another audiotape surfaced a few days later, urging Iraqis to show their dissatisfaction with the American occupation by "writing on walls, hindering the work of the

The Text of Saddam's Letter

The following is an excerpt from a letter allegedly written by Saddam Hussein. It is signed by Saddam and is dated April 28, 2003. It was published by the London-based Arabic newspaper *Al-Quds al-Arabi* and can be found on the BBC News Web site.

28 April 2003, from Saddam Hussein to the great Iraqi people, the sons of the Arab and Islamic nation and the honorable ones everywhere, God's peace, mercy and blessings be with you. . . .

O sons of our great people, rise against the occupier. . . .

There are no priorities other than the expulsion of the infidel, criminal, murderous and cowardly occupier with whom not a single honorable person, only the traitors and agents, shook hands. I tell you that . . . God is with you because you are fighting the infidels and defending your rights. . . .

Forget everything and resist the occupation. The sin begins when there are priorities other than the occupier and his expulsion. . . . Those who have stood against Iraq and plotted against it will not enjoy peace at the hands of the United States.

Greetings to everyone who resists, to every honorable Iraqi citizen and to every woman, child and old man in our great Iraq. . . .

Protect your possessions, districts and schools. Boycott the occupier; boycott him because this is the duty of Islam, religion and the homeland.

Long live the great Iraq and its people. . . .

God is Great. Let the accursed be cursed.

occupation, boycotting trade with them and demonstrating." The tape continued, "I am speaking especially to the youths who have faith in God, and who still possess missiles and grenade launchers."[28] In November 2003 another tape reportedly made by Saddam was broadcast on Arab television. In the tape, Saddam called for holy war against America, the killing of "those who are installed by foreign armies"[29] (a reference to the Iraqi Governing Council), and the return of the Baath Party to power in Iraq. Saddam was leaving no doubt that he wanted to regain control of Iraq.

As the United States soon discovered, managing postwar Iraq proved a much harder task than winning the war. Due to both the lack of preparedness and the immense difficulty of the job, American forces were unable to bring immediate order to Iraq, and a growing state of chaos and fear persisted.

Chapter 3

Growing Terrorism and Resistance

By late fall of 2003 a disturbing new phenomenon had developed in Iraq—Iraqi guerrilla fighters began attacking U.S. troops and their supporters as they tried to stabilize the country. Eventually, attacks included shocking terrorist bombings of UN and humanitarian aid headquarters as well as others assisting the United States in the reconstruction process. The growing guerrilla war sabotaged U.S. efforts to rebuild the country and caused many Iraqis to fear for their lives and their future. The violence also brought into question America's ability to bring stability, democracy, and prosperity to the Iraqi people.

Guerrilla Attacks on U.S. Troops and Officials

The attacks on U.S. soldiers began with hit-and-run attacks during the summer of 2003. They were concentrated in areas of Iraq considered supportive of Saddam and his Baath Party followers. Cities such as Tikrit, Saddam's hometown, and small towns such as Fallujah and Ramadi became the frequent scenes of violent, bloody attacks on U.S. soldiers.

By early July 2003, U.S. military commanders confirmed that increasingly sophisticated explosive devices were being used against American forces. Rocket-propelled grenades and bombs became the weapons of choice for the militants, who repeatedly attacked U.S. soldiers, military vehicles, and military-related sites. These attacks often killed both soldiers and innocent Iraqi bystanders.

On November 2, 2003, insurgents shot down an American helicopter near Fallujah using shoulder-held antiaircraft missiles. The assault killed sixteen soldiers and wounded twenty others, most on their way out of Iraq to take much-needed leaves. Shortly thereafter hostile fire brought down two more American helicopters in the northern city of Mosul, killing seventeen American soldiers and injuring five others.

Insurgents also appeared to target high-level American officials in Iraq. An attack in

October, for example, hit a hotel where an important visitor was staying—Paul D. Wolfowitz, the U.S. deputy secretary of defense and one of the leading architects of the war against Iraq. Later, strikes came close to hitting both L. Paul Bremer, America's civilian administrator for Iraq, and General John Abizaid, the top U.S. military commander for the Iraqi occupation.

Attacks Against Iraqis

Soon the attacks escalated to include Iraqi policemen and others who were cooperating with U.S. occupation forces. On July 5, 2003, for example, guerrillas bombed a graduation ceremony for the first American-trained class for a new police force in Iraq. Seven Iraqi police recruits were killed. Another police station was bombed within a few days. In early September a car bomb exploded outside the Iraqi police academy in central Baghdad, leaving one person dead

U.S. deputy secretary of defense Paul Wolfowitz (center) was unhurt when insurgents attacked his hotel in Mosul in July 2003.

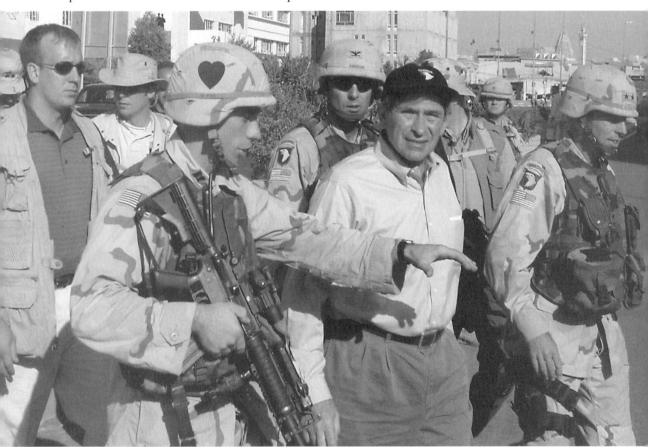

and twenty-eight wounded. Attacks against Iraqi police officers and other Iraqis who appeared to be working with U.S. officials then became more frequent. Dozens of policemen were killed in bombings, including a senior Iraqi police official who was shot and killed on his way to pray at a mosque with his young son.

The bomb attacks also targeted high-profile Iraqis who supported the Americans. Ayatollah Mohammad Baqir al-Hakim, for instance, a leading Shia cleric and an important U.S. ally in Iraq, was killed on August 29, 2003, along with about eighty others outside the Imam Ali shrine, the holiest shrine in Shia Islam. In mid-September insurgents even attacked a member of the Iraqi Governing Council, Akila al-Hashemi. She was shot in the street on her way to work. The Iraqi Governing Council called for three days of national mourning and issued a statement: "[Al-Hashemi] fell as a martyr on the path of freedom and democracy to build this great nation. . . . She died at the hands of a clique of infidels and cunning people who only know darkness."[30] The targeting of high-profile Iraqis continued. On May 17, 2004, the president of IGC, Ezzedine Salim, was killed by a suicide bomber.

The attacks put further pressure on both Iraqis and Americans. Iraqis who wanted to cooperate with U.S. forces became terrified to do so. The American plans for rebuilding and exiting the country, however, depended on enlisting the help of Iraqis so the United States could eventually turn the country back over to them. As attacks on cooperating Iraqis escalated, the U.S. forces had an increasingly difficult time convincing Iraqis that it was safe to join their side. This situation greatly paralyzed the rebuilding efforts and put further strain on the occupation.

Aware that they were succeeding in preventing Americans and Iraqis from uniting in common cause, the insurgents continued their attacks. They often chose targets that offered little or no resistance, known as soft targets. In early October 2003, for example, an insurgent set off a massive car bomb in a crowd of Iraqi policemen, killing eight and injuring more than forty. Later that month bombers attacked a hotel in Baghdad used by members of the Iraqi Governing Council and many Americans. A similar bomb in a separate attack killed two Iraqi police officers and six civilians. Other incidents included rocket attacks launched from donkey carts against the Iraqi oil ministry.

Attacks eventually focused on a particular group of Iraqis—the Shias, a sect of Muslims. In the early months of 2004 several deadly attacks were coordinated against Shias, who had long been targets of violence in Iraq. The worst attacks occurred on March 2, 2004, and were meant to coincide with the Shia holiday of Ashura. This is a celebration in which Shia Muslims from all over the world come to the Iraqi city of Karbala to visit the tomb of Imam Hussein, an important figure in Shiism.

As hundreds of thousands of religious pilgrims gathered in cities around Iraq to celebrate the holiday, multiple suicide bombers struck. In Baghdad three suicide bombers detonated weapons in and around shrines, killing worshippers. Meanwhile, in Karbala at least five powerful blasts struck crowds of pilgrims who had packed the streets and shrines for the Ashura ceremony. Witnesses described complete anarchy, watching as terrified worshipers desperately sought escape from the carnage. Blood and body parts were reportedly seen scattered in the street and spattered against the walls of the sacred shrines. In all, more than 140 people were killed in the deadliest day of violence since the occupation of Iraq began.

Although it is not entirely clear who was behind these attacks, it is believed the violence was intended to divide an already fractured Iraq. Indeed, some insurgents may be looking to spark a civil war between Iraqi Shias and Sunnis. These two groups frequently vie for power, and each hopes to become the dominant authority in the new Iraqi government. The attacks on Shias, therefore, may be among the first violent manifestations of that power struggle coming to the streets of Iraq.

The attacks also put American forces in a terribly difficult position. Prior to the Ashura attacks, many Shias had insisted that the American troops not be present for the sensitive celebration. However, after the attacks American forces were criticized for not providing adequate security for the holiday. As Adnan Pachachi, a member of the Iraqi Governing Council, put it, "For months, people have been insisting that the Americans leave the cities . . . and when they finally do that, people blame the Americans for not protecting them."[31] In a way, one of the gravest consequences of the Ashura attacks might be that Iraqis will stop looking to American troops to protect them and will start their own private militias. If this happens, it will be even more difficult to control the violence and chaos that plague postwar Iraq.

Attacks Against Humanitarian Agencies

In yet another disturbing twist, the insurgency attacked international humanitarian organizations, targeting agencies whose goal is to improve the lives of civilians by distributing clothes, food, medicine, or providing other help. For example, on August 19, 2003, the UN headquarters in Baghdad was attacked. A suicide bomber drove a cement truck into the side of the compound, blowing it up. The explosion destroyed the building, scattered body parts throughout the area, and left twenty-two dead and at least one hundred wounded. Among the dead was Sergio Vieira de Mello, the UN special representative to Iraq. The UN had no troops in Iraq at this time, so its presence was nonmilitary; the attack thus sent ripples of fear and disbelief around the world. After the attack, the United Nations pulled much of its staff from Iraq, leaving only a small number of non-Iraqi workers behind. Its exit left many in shock and with great concerns for the future. It also indicated that the situation in Iraq was spiraling out of control.

In late October 2003 such suicide attacks grew more frequent. Attacks that month

Shia Muslims self-inflict wounds in observance of the holiday of Ashura in 2004. Suicide bombers struck during the celebration, killing more than 140 people.

killed a total of 34 people and wounded another 224. A spate of bombs exploded across Baghdad—the offices of the International Committee of the Red Cross was one target. Afterward, the Red Cross closed its offices in Basra and Baghdad. Other aid agencies, frightened by the violence, followed suit. These organizations had begun a variety of aid efforts, providing everything from food and medicine to school repairs. The loss of these humanitarian organizations left Iraq without the help it sorely needed to rebuild its society after the war. For example, the pullout of UN staff caused an early shutdown of northern Iraq's oil-for-food program, which had provided many Iraqis with food and other necessities.

Attacks on U.S. Allies

The Iraqi insurgents also targeted America's international allies. On August 7, 2003, for example, a powerful bomb was detonated outside the Jordanian embassy in Baghdad. The car bomb killed at least eight people and wounded more than thirty others. On October 14, 2003, amid controversy about whether Turkey would send troops to Iraq to assist U.S. forces, a bomb exploded close to the Turkish embassy in Baghdad, leaving two people wounded.

Guerrillas launched an even deadlier attack on November 13, 2003, when they exploded a car bomb in the courtyard of an Italian paramilitary police headquarters in southern Iraq. This attack killed 18 Italians and at least 9 Iraqis and wounded more than 105. In addition, later explosions targeted companies in Turkey owned by America's coalition partner, Britain—one at the British consulate and the other at a British international bank—killing 27 and wounding more than 400.

In late November 2003 resistance fighters carried out more bloody ambushes against several American allies. On November 30, Iraqi guerrillas shot rocket-propelled grenades at two cars carrying eight Spanish intelligence officers in Mahmudiya, south of Baghdad,

The Insurgents' Arsenal

The insurgents fighting American forces in Iraq appear to be well funded. It is believed their money comes from large pools of cash stolen by Saddam before the war. According to a former Iraqi minister, Saddam may have skimmed tens of billions of dollars from Iraqi oil revenues and stashed it in foreign bank accounts. Indeed, Saddam reportedly took 5 percent of oil revenues from 1972 until 1990—an amount that would total about $31 billion, enough to fund a long guerrilla war. U.S. officials believe that these funds are being used to fund the insurgency.

The insurgents also appear to have access to large supplies of explosives and weapons—most of them from Saddam's large weapons stockpiles. Indeed, virtually all the suicide bombings and attacks on American soldiers and Iraqis were carried out with material taken from Iraqi weapons sites. The U.S. military estimated that Iraq had close to 1 million tons of weapons and ammunition scattered around the country. Because of their number, these weapons sites could not be quickly located or destroyed by U.S. troops. For the same

reason, they remained mostly unguarded, allowing Iraqi fighters to plunder them at will.

The biggest concern was the insurgents' apparent access to a large number of shoulder-fired antiaircraft missiles that were part of Saddam's weapons arsenal, which U.S. forces could not find. The missing missiles, which could number in the hundreds, caused U.S. officials to delay reopening Baghdad International Airport to commercial traffic even though it has been rebuilt, the runways have been repaired, and it has a functioning air traffic control system. Most frightening, insurgents repeatedly attempted to use the antiaircraft missiles against military planes. These attacks were not successful, indicating that the missile users had little training. In August 2003, for example, one report said that there were twenty-one attempts to bring down coalition aircraft. The U.S. forces in Iraq desperately tried to locate the missiles, and through searches and rewards, they had retrieved hundreds. However, officials worried about the missiles that remained unaccounted for.

killing seven of them. That same day, in Tikrit, guerrillas killed two Japanese diplomats in an ambush and shot two South Korean civilians who were working for a South Korean company assisting Iraq with electrical repairs.

Attacks Appear Coordinated and Goal Oriented

Insurgent attacks increased in both numbers and range. U.S. military officials confirmed, for instance, that the average number of daily attacks in Iraq had increased from about thirty-five attacks each day in October 2003 to a peak of about fifty per day in November 2003. The attacks also became increasingly bolder, employing more sophisticated weaponry (such as antiaircraft missiles), killing larger numbers of victims, and branching out to areas in northern and southern Iraq. Despite the fact that the United States estimated that guerrilla forces numbered only about five thousand, they seemed to be highly organized.

As the attacks mounted, they seemed to show a clear strategy, suggesting coordination and central control. American commanders themselves agreed that the intensifying attacks showed a progressively higher degree of planning, coordination, and intelligence gathering on the part of the Iraqi fighters, even approaching the level of the Iraqi military organization seen during the war. All of the attacks were clearly part of an effort to destabilize Iraq and drive out the Americans, but no one was certain who the insurgents were.

By October 2003 Bush administration officials began suggesting that the attackers

were likely a combination of followers of Saddam and foreign terrorists. As President Bush explained in an October 28 news conference:

> We're trying to determine the nature of who these people were, but . . . I would assume that they're either/or—and probably both—Baathists and foreign terrorists. The Baathists try to create chaos and fear because they realize that a free Iraq will deny them the excessive privileges they had under Saddam. The foreign terrorists are trying to create conditions of fear and retreat because they fear a free and peaceful state in the midst of a part of the world where terror has found recruits. [32]

U.S. officials also indicated that the attackers were assisted by criminals who were being paid to carry out attacks.

The resistance strategy, U.S. officials said, may have been developed and coordinated long before the first American soldier set foot in Iraq. In November 2003, for example, interrogations of former senior Iraqi officials in U.S. custody revealed that the broad outlines of the guerrilla campaign were drawn up by the Iraqi intelligence service before the war. Indications suggested that this resistance plan was now being implemented, organized, and financed by Saddam and his followers.

An Iraqi Jihad—Foreign Fighters in Iraq

It was also suspected that foreign militants were sneaking into Iraq across the Syrian and

U.S. officials believe that Saddam Hussein planned the Iraqi guerrilla resistance campaign long before the March 2003 coalition invasion.

Iranian borders to fight U.S. troops. Indeed, some reports suggested that a wave of Muslim militants was headed to Iraq, in response to the call of terrorists such as Osama bin Laden for Muslims to join a jihad, or holy war, against the American-led occupation. Some even speculated that Saddam and his supporters were coordinating with these for-

eign terrorists. In September 2003 President Bush stated, "These killers . . . have made Iraq the central front in the war on terror." [33]

However, it was difficult for the U.S. military to determine the identity and intentions of the fighters because only a few of them had been arrested for involvement in the attacks. Bush administration officials estimated that the number of foreign fighters in Iraq could be as large as one to three thousand, but they could not be sure. Although their numbers were uncertain, it was clear that the Iraqi insurgency was using terrorist tactics against the American occupation. U.S. officials, for example, noted that the Iraqi fighters were operating under a structure of loosely coordinated "cells," similar to the organization of the terrorist group al Qaeda, and using terrorist tactics such as suicide bombers.

In early 2004 evidence seemed to confirm a foreign terrorist element in Iraq. On January 29, 2004, for example, U.S. forces arrested Hassan Ghul, a top al Qaeda operative, as he tried to enter northern Iraq. U.S. military commander Ricardo Sanchez explains, "The capture of Ghul is pretty strong proof that [al Qaeda] is trying to gain a foothold here to continue their murderous campaigns. Ghul's capture is great news for the Iraqis, for the coalition and for the international community's war against terrorism." [34]

The arrest of Ghul, in turn, produced information about another al Qaeda terrorist—Abu Musab al-Zarqawi. U.S. officials had long suspected that al-Zarqawi was in Iraq, but they learned from Ghul that he likely was involved in at least three major car bombings in Iraq, including attacks on the UN headquarters in Baghdad, a Shia mosque in Najaf, and an Italian police headquarters.

Also in January, American officials found a document confirmed to have been written by al-Zarqawi that suggested collaboration between al Qaeda and the Iraqi insurgents. The document complained that Iraqi fighters were having problems gaining support among Iraqis and failing to scare the Americans into leaving Iraq; it suggested that turning Iraq's ethnic groups against each other and promoting a civil war was the best way to undermine U.S. efforts there. In the document, al-Zarqawi asked senior leaders of al Qaeda for help in mounting attacks on the Shia ethnic group in Iraq. Such attacks, the document argued, could prompt the Shias to counterattack against another Iraqi ethnic group, the Sunnis, and start a civil war that would help rally Iraqis to support the insurgents' battle against the U.S. occupation. Hoping to stop this plan, U.S. officials in February 2004 offered a reward of $10 million for information leading to the arrest and conviction of al-Zarqawi.

A Deadly Insurgency

In addition to creating continuing instability in Iraq and killing large numbers of Iraqis, the insurgency caused an increasing number of American deaths. Indeed, more U.S. soldiers died during the postwar guerrilla attacks than during what was officially considered the war in Iraq. By the end of April 2004, for instance, a total of 793 U.S. service members had died (and 3,466 had been injured) since the beginning of military operations in Iraq. The majority of these deaths occurred during the insurgency, which began after May 1, 2003, when President Bush declared that major combat operations in

Supporters of Saddam demonstrate against the U.S. invasion. Militant Muslims believe it is their duty to wage a holy war against the U.S. occupation.

Iraq had ended. Only 138 deaths occurred during the war.

Even more alarming, the number of American deaths was on the upswing; casualty numbers had increased, not decreased, since the summer of 2003. In November, the bloodiest month for American forces, 81 U.S. soldiers died, compared with 73 in April, the month that the United States invaded Iraq. In addition, as of November 2003, about 2,000 U.S. soldiers had been injured by hostile action and hundreds more died as a result of accidents or non-hostile forces. Allied forces from countries such as Britain, Italy, Spain, Denmark, Ukraine, and Poland also suffered casualties, although in much smaller numbers than the United States.

The growing number of casualties worried Americans and spawned skepticism about America's ability to succeed in rebuilding the country because U.S. forces were unable to stop the insurgency attacks. In the United States, some critics began comparing postwar Iraq to the war in Vietnam—another war in which America fought terrorists and guerrilla fighters, and one that was ultimately lost after many thousands of American casualties.

Efforts to Curb the Violence

To curb the increasing violence, the United States stepped up its military activities in Iraq and called up additional troops.

As more and more suspected insurgents were rounded up, the U.S. military detained them for questioning in various facilities around Iraq. Some detention centers were makeshift camps in the desert; others were fortified prisons formerly used as torture centers during Saddam's regime. There, U.S. personnel held and interrogated Iraqis suspected of taking part in or having information about the insurgency.

Although coalition forces were bound by internationally accepted conventions to treat prisoners humanely, in May 2004 it came to light that terrible abuses had been committed in at least one American-controlled Iraqi detention facility. Photographs surfaced showing U.S. soldiers cheerfully posing beside Iraqi prisoners who had been stripped naked and forced into uncomfortable positions or stacked in piles. Other photographs showed naked Iraqis being attacked by police dogs and otherwise terrorized or humiliated. Even more disturbing reports described the sexual abuse of inmates by soldiers, including rape.

It was unclear if a few corrupt soldiers had acted on their own initiative or if the atrocities had been sanctioned by high-ranking military officials. In any case, the abuse of prisoners was decried around the world. Shocked and outraged responses called into question the morality of the American mission in Iraq, whose stated goal had been to end the era of torture Iraqis had suffered under Saddam.

President Bush condemned the prisoner abuse as being inconsistent with American values and the honorable record of the armed forces in Iraq. Congress launched an inquiry into the scandal, vowing to bring

The Insurgency Continues

The capture of Saddam Hussein caused many Iraqis to celebrate, but it also caused many to wonder whether the insurgency in Iraq would continue without Saddam's leadership. U.S. officials predicted that attacks would continue, and that they even might increase as the Iraqi fighters tried to show that they would not be stopped by the loss of Saddam. In December 2003, for example, President Bush cautioned that Saddam's capture might not mean the end of violence in Iraq.

He was proven right when a car bomb exploded on December 14, 2003, just twelve hours after Saddam's capture. The attack killed seventeen. It was quickly followed by similar car-bomb attacks on police stations in Baghdad on December 15, 2003, killing six Iraqi police officers and wounding twenty others. In the following weeks, however, U.S. military officials claimed that insurgent attacks against coalition forces had declined to an average of about eighteen per day, compared to twenty-three per day in the weeks before Saddam's capture. In addition, U.S. forces said more Iraqis seemed willing to provide intelligence about the insurgency. Nevertheless, insurgent attacks on American forces and other targets in Iraq continued in 2004 with no end in sight.

those responsible to justice. These efforts, however, did not quell the anger of the Iraqi people. Indeed, the insurgency intensified after the abuse scandal came to light, as militants vowed revenge on military personnel and American civilians alike.

Active-duty troops were rotated into Iraq to relieve soldiers who had been there since the start of the war, and fifteen thousand noncombat National Guard troops from Arkansas, North Carolina, and Washington were activated to assist with operations in Iraq. In ad-

dition, the Pentagon notified another forty-three thousand Reserve and National Guard troops that they may be called in the future for yearlong duty in Iraq. Meanwhile, although overall allied help was disappointing, a few U.S. allies, such as Poland and Spain, began to send limited numbers of troops to Iraq.

It was also thought that the violence could be stopped if security forces, such as police, could be turned over to the Iraqis. Putting an Iraqi face on security efforts in Iraq, U.S. officials hoped, might stem some of the violence because insurgents might be less likely to attack other Iraqis. In addition, U.S. commanders thought that Iraqis, who are fluent in the language and familiar with local customs, might have access to better intelligence information than U.S. troops. U.S. forces therefore began recruiting and training a new forty-thousand-member Iraqi army as well as a seven-thousand-member Iraqi civil defense force and a new police force. As of late 2003, five thousand civil militia soldiers were already working with U.S. troops, and thirty-four thousand police officers had been trained. However, U.S. officials acknowledged that it would still be a long time before Iraqis could fully take over security duties.

Yet another way America responded to the increasing violence was by speeding up the transfer of political power to Iraqis. In November 2003 the United States abandoned the administration's previous game plan—drafting a constitution, followed by elections, followed by American withdrawal—

and announced that it would hold elections in the first half of 2004 and turn civilian authority over to a temporary government by July that same year. The administration hoped this plan, by showing Iraqis that the United States was moving quickly to allow Iraqi self-rule, would help reduce support for the attacks on American forces.

American Raids on Insurgents

It also became a priority to root out Iraqi militants and put down the insurgency so the work of rebuilding the country could carry on smoothly. U.S. forces therefore conducted major raids and house-to-house searches in areas suspected of housing Iraqi insurgents. Some of these raids were highly successful in catching persons believed to be either insurgents or their supporters. One such operation in July 2003, for example, involved 143 raids throughout Iraq. Almost seven hundred suspected Baathists were detained, sixty-four of whom were considered important Saddam supporters. These raids continued as months passed, disrupting insurgent strongholds and sometimes yielding important clues about insurgent activities.

The Alienation of Iraqi Citizens

The U.S. military raids designed to combat the Iraqi insurgents, along with the prisoner abuse scandal, soon alienated many ordinary Iraqis who were often caught up in the raids. The American military's large and aggressive sweeps of towns and villages looking for militants, for example, also often rounded up several hundred Iraqis who had done

nothing wrong. Iraqis also complained that U.S. soldiers were insensitive to Iraqi culture and traditions as they conducted the raids. For example, U.S. soldiers would disturb women and girls at night when they were not modestly dressed, as Islam requires. As one U.S. defense official explained, "To a lot of Iraqis, we're no longer the guys who threw out Saddam, but the ones who are busting down doors and barging in on their wives and daughters."[35]

Indeed, a secret report by the U.S. Central Intelligence Agency (CIA) released in November 2003 suggested that the United States was beginning to lose the support and faith of Iraqis who had initially supported the U.S. effort, creating an even more fertile environment for the anti-American guerrilla war. For instance, in Mosul, a northern Iraqi town in which U.S. forces enjoyed great support early in the war, the tide of opinion seemed to turn despite a highly successful U.S. effort there to rebuild roads, schools, and public buildings. Raad Khairy al-Barhawi, a Mosul city councilman, explained the diminishing goodwill by describing an incident that involved a local cleric. The cleric was detained by U.S. troops on suspicion of encouraging attacks against the Americans in his sermons. Al-Barhawi claimed that American troops handcuffed, hooded, and slapped the cleric before releasing him, angering townspeople who respected the man. Al-Barhawi says, "I am not defending the cleric, but he was humiliated in public. . . . Do you realize what he is going to say in his sermons now?"[36]

As a result, the U.S. military tried to carry out more precise and less intrusive attacks rather than broad military sweeps. U.S. troops began singling out a specific house suspected of being a hideout for militants instead of targeting a whole block or area. However, in the face of escalating violence American forces were forced to resume an aggressive strategy in order to regain the upper hand against the Iraqi guerrilla fighters. For example, late in 2003 U.S. forces used air strikes, tanks, and Apache helicopter gunships against insurgents and their suspected convoys and bases in Iraq. In addition, the U.S. Air Force used some of the largest weapons in its inventory, including one-thousand- to two-thousand-pound satellite-guided bombs,

An Iraqi man working with U.S. Marines kicks arrested looters. Such harsh treatment of Iraqis helped erode popular support for the U.S. occupation.

to attack targets suspected of being guerrilla strongholds. The U.S. military called the new initiative Operation Iron Hammer.

In early 2004 the United States continued to struggle against a small group of guerrillas who, with ample funding and weapons, appeared to be winning a low-level war of resistance to the U.S. occupation, continuing the chaos and insecurity in Iraq.

U.S. Forces Capture Saddam

Just before 2003 ended, America scored a huge symbolic victory in its battle against the insurgents: It captured the elusive Saddam. Acting on a tip from a member of Saddam's tribal clan, U.S. forces found Saddam on December 13, dirty and disheveled, hiding in an eight-foot-wide hole in the ground under an isolated farmhouse near Tikrit. As Major General Raymond T. Odierno, the commander of the U.S. Army's Fourth Infantry Division, told reporters, "He was just caught like a rat."[37]

Although Saddam was armed with a pistol, he did not fight back but surrendered meekly. Two AK-47 rifles and $775,000 in cash were found nearby. U.S. military officials also found a briefcase containing documents linking him to the insurgency. The documents confirmed the existence of insurgent "cells," or groups, and clarified that the guerrilla leaders were doling out funding to fighters from a central pool of cash. Based on the information found with Saddam, U.S. troops were able to capture several top regime figures believed to be part of the insurgency.

Soon after his capture the United States released a video of Saddam in custody, showing him undergoing a medical exam conducted by American doctors. In the video Saddam appeared with a long beard, uncut hair, and looking old, tired, and beaten —a shadow of the powerful Arab leader he once was. Iraqis and Arabs were shocked and humiliated, both by Saddam's appearance and especially by his failure to fight; Saddam had always portrayed himself as a strong leader who would fight to the end, and many wanted him to at least die fighting.

In a televised address, President Bush said of the capture, "In the history of Iraq, a dark and painful era is over. . . . A hopeful day has arrived. All Iraqis can now come together and reject violence and build a new Iraq."[38] However, Bush and other U.S. officials were careful to say that insurgent attacks in Iraq were likely to continue. Saddam's detention may have deprived the insurgents of a rallying symbol, but they were expected to keep fighting the American rebuilding effort. Also, given Saddam's disheveled state and the fact that he was constantly on the move to hide from U.S. forces, it seemed unlikely that he was actively coordinating the resistance. The real guerrilla leaders, therefore, were probably still on the loose and likely to continue the battle against U.S. forces.

★ Chapter 4 ★

Iraq: An American Responsibility

Because the United States had fought the war against Iraq virtually alone, it insisted on full control over the rebuilding process. However, with control came responsibility, and the United States soon learned that other nations, especially those who opposed the war in the first place, were unwilling to contribute troops or reconstruction aid as long as the United States insisted on running the show. Thus, the United States shouldered almost the full burden of postwar reconstruction costs, which quickly ballooned to enormous amounts.

The United States Is Granted Full Authority in Iraq

After its military victory, the United States quickly sought UN approval to occupy and rebuild Iraq. Such approval, U.S. officials believed, would help legitimize the U.S.-led war; in other words, make the war valid in the eyes of the world. It would also allow America to decide how to develop Iraq's political and economic systems.

On May 22, 2003, therefore, the United States (and its main ally, Britain) pushed for and won UN Resolution 1483, which granted an international mandate to the U.S.-led coalition to occupy and rebuild Iraq. It was a major diplomatic victory for the United States, giving what had been a controversial war international legitimacy. Most importantly, the resolution gave the United States what it most desired—control and authority over Iraq's political development and its billions of dollars in annual oil revenues. This authority, under the terms of the resolution, would end once a representative, internationally recognized Iraqi government took power in Iraq. Pleased with this outcome, President Bush praised the resolution as a sign of international unity, stating, "The nations of the world have demonstrated their unity in their commitment to help the Iraqi people on the path to a better future." [39]

The United States had to go to great lengths to win the resolution. For example, countries such as France and Russia, which had bitterly opposed the war, were not inclined just a few weeks later to suddenly help the United States as it tried to legitimize its actions. Furthermore, the United States had to allay the fears of many countries that were worried that the U.S. occupation could inflame anti-American sentiments and create instability rather than peace in the region. As a result, the United States made several concessions to obtain broad support for the resolution.

To help convince Russia to support the resolution, for example, the United States agreed Russia could receive roughly $1.5 billion in already-approved UN contracts between Russian companies and the old Iraqi regime. France's concerns were different; it wanted to see a UN presence established in Iraq. Therefore, to gain French support for the resolution, the United States agreed to a UN special representative who would help with the political reconstruction of Iraq. Sergio Vieira de Mello, the widely respected UN high commissioner for human rights, was later appointed to this position. In addition, U.S. negotiators agreed to allow the United Nations (along with international financial organizations like the World Bank, the International Monetary Fund, and the Arab Fund for Social and Economic Development) to sit on an international advisory board that would monitor and audit the U.S. expenditures of oil revenues in Iraq.

These concessions helped convince many countries that had been against the war to vote for the resolution, thereby entrusting postwar Iraq to the United States. Many countries were also motivated by a desire to help the people of Iraq by moving the rebuilding process forward. As the German ambassador, Gunter Pleuger, remarked, "The war that we did not want . . . has taken place . . . we cannot undo history. We are now in a situation where we have to take action for the sake of the Iraqi people."[40]

Sergio Vieira de Mello, a UN commissioner for human rights, was appointed as a special representative to help with the political reconstruction of Iraq.

A Lack of International Troops

Following the vote on UN Resolution 1483, the United States hoped it could also persuade other countries to take a hand in stabilizing and rebuilding Iraq. Indeed, the resolution specifically called on UN members "to assist the people of Iraq in their efforts to reform their institutions and rebuild their country."[41] Because so many countries had voted in favor of the resolution, U.S. officials believed these nations would soon send troops to help U.S. forces tackle the first enormous job—restoring order in Iraq.

As time passed, however, very little international military aid was provided by other countries, and American troops far outnumbered soldiers from any other country. In July 2003, for example, 147,000 U.S. soldiers served in Iraq. Some twenty-four other countries had sent troops to Iraq, but they totaled only about thirteen-thousand non-American troops, most of them British. Most countries, such as Hungary, Bulgaria, Honduras, El Salvador, Ukraine, Slovakia, Denmark, and Spain, sent only a small number of troops.

To encourage more countries to send troops, on September 23, 2003, President Bush argued in a speech at the United Nations that it was important to stabilize and rebuild Iraq. A democratic Iraq, he said, would transform the Middle East, and this would produce benefits for the whole world:

Millions will see that freedom, equality and material progress are possible at the heart of the Middle East. Leaders in the region will face the clearest evidence that free institutions and open societies are the only path to long-term national success and dignity. And a transformed Middle East would benefit the entire world by undermining the ideologies that export violence to other lands. Iraq as a dictatorship had great power to destabilize the Middle East. Iraq as a democracy will have great power to inspire the Middle East.[42]

The United States, however, insisted that any troops sent by other countries must operate under U.S. military command. Many nations did not like this stipulation; they did not want their troops operating under U.S. control. Russia, for instance, said it would send troops only if the United Nations took over military command and only if a specific date was set for ending the U.S. occupation and handing over power to the Iraqis. Similarly, India, which the United States hoped would send seventeen thousand troops, decided it could not send its soldiers unless they operated under the control of the United Nations. Pakistan and Turkey also showed the same type of reluctance. Indeed, virtually no other countries—except for some in eastern Europe, such as Poland—were willing to place their troops under American command in Iraq.

Countries such as Germany and France explained that they did not want to share the burden of the U.S. occupation when the United States did not want to share any power. As one diplomat put it, "We are not here to serve as a fig leaf [that is, a cover] for aggression. . . . The U.S. does not want to share power in Iraq. It does not want to share authority. All it wants to share are the casualties and the costs. That is a very brutal, one-sided game, and we should not be playing it."[43] Indeed, as *New York Times* columnist Bob Herbert explains:

> There [was] a widespread feeling at the U.N. that the policies of the United States—its invasion and occupation of Iraq . . . and its frequently contemptuous attitude toward the U.N. in particular and international cooperation in general—have made the Middle East and parts of the rest of the world substantially more dangerous, rather than less.[44]

After intensive U.S. pressure, the most that the United States achieved was a UN resolution on the future of Iraq—Resolution 1511—which passed on October 16, 2003, and provided only symbolic statements urging countries to support Iraq's rebuilding. Russia, France, and Germany made clear in a public announcement that their support for the resolution did not mean that they would be providing troops or any more aid than what they had already given. Likewise, countries such as Turkey, India, Pakistan, and Japan, which U.S. officials were counting on to provide more troops, either canceled or delayed their plans to do so. The United States, therefore, was left to carry the military burden in Iraq virtually alone.

A Lack of Money to Rebuild Iraq

The U.S. insistence on full control in postwar Iraq also made many countries reluctant to contribute reconstruction money to rebuilding efforts. Only a handful of countries contributed anything significant. Britain (which contributed $439 million) and Spain (which contributed $300 million) became the only European Union (EU) countries to step forward with additional funding above a relatively small combined-EU contribution. The EU, representing fifteen European countries, approved a mere $233 million in reconstruction aid for Iraq, a figure that amounted to only about 1 percent of the $20 billion donated by the United States in reconstruction aid. A few other wealthy countries, such as Japan ($1.5 billion), South Korea ($200 million), and Canada ($260 million), came forward with pledges, but the bulk of the funding was supplied by the United States.

U.S. officials hoped that an international fund-raising conference scheduled for October 23–24, 2003, in Madrid, Spain, would provide the funds the United States believed would be necessary to rebuild Iraq. In particular, American policy makers hoped Arab countries that were U.S. allies, such as the United Arab Emirates, Kuwait, Qatar, and Saudi Arabia, would offer substantial help. The United States and the World Bank estimated that a total of $55 billion was needed to rebuild Iraq through 2007. After subtracting $20 billion to be contributed by the United States and $5 billion expected to come from Iraqi oil revenues, $35 billion in additional contributions needed to be pledged at Madrid.

At the Madrid donors' conference, however, donations fell substantially short of this figure. The conference produced pledges totaling only $13 billion over five years. Even more discouraging, roughly two-thirds of the aid pledged came in the form of loans rather than money grants. The United States had strongly urged donors to give money instead of loaning it, claiming Iraq needed aid, not more debt. Also, most of the loan amount was donated from international organizations such as the World Bank and the International Monetary Fund, not from individual countries.

Adding to the disappointment, wealthy Arab countries did not come through with the large number of grants that the United States had wanted. Their reluctance was attributed to their opposition to the U.S. war and occupation of Iraq as well as other long-held grievances against the United States. In the end, the United Arab Emirates offered only about $200 million, Saudi Arabia offered $1 billion in loans, and Kuwait pledged $500 million.

Nevertheless, U.S. secretary of state Colin Powell tried to put the best face on the results, calling the Madrid meeting "a very successful conference."[45] Powell, however, admitted that the monies received were short of what the United States had expected. The only bright spot was a prediction from a team of World Bank economists, who concluded that the amount of money pledged at Madrid would easily support Iraq through 2004.

Kofi Annan Criticizes U.S. Policy

Following the bombing of the UN headquarters in Iraq on August 19, 2003, the UN secretary-general, Kofi Annan, gave a much-publicized speech that revealed the degree of animosity between the United Nations and the United States. Annan criticized the U.S. policy of preemption that led to the U.S. invasion of Iraq. In a clear reference to President Bush's policy, Annan dismissed the notion that countries have the right to use force preemptively. He also argued that the policy challenged the founding principles of the United Nations. By this he meant that the purpose of the United Nations was to maintain peace in the world and to resolve international conflicts diplomatically.

Indeed, Annan said the preemption policy "represents a fundamental challenge to the principles on which, however imperfectly, world peace and stability have rested for the last fifty-eight years."

UN secretary-general Kofi Annan condemned the invasion of Iraq.

Many argue that for subsequent years, however, the United States must somehow find a way to reestablish friendships with nations it has alienated. *New York Times* columnist Thomas L. Friedman, for example, argues that America has to have friends to succeed in Iraq: "Iraq is the most audacious nation-building project America has ever engaged in. But to succeed, we need partners— not only to help, but to provide legitimacy so we can sustain it. Right now, though, we are operating in a context of enormous global animosity. We are dancing alone."[46]

The War's Cost for America

Because Iraq had become America's responsibility, massive amounts of U.S. taxpayer dollars were needed to pay for stabilizing and rebuilding the country. The true cost to Americans was revealed in September 2003, when President Bush asked Congress for the staggering sum of $87 billion in emergency spending for military operations and reconstruction, most of which would be spent in Iraq. (Portions of the amount were designated for Afghanistan, another country the United States was in the midst of rebuilding.) Bush justified the expenditure by asserting that Iraq had now become "the central front" in the campaign against terrorism, and that defeating terrorists in Iraq "will take time, and require sacrifice."[47]

In October 2003, both houses of the U.S. Congress approved the $87-billion package. About $71 billion was earmarked for Iraq: $51 billion for military and intelligence operations and $20 billion for reconstruction. This amount is in addition to the $79 billion approved by Congress earlier to pay the war costs for 2003. This made America's total costs for the war and its aftermath, as of 2004, close to $150 billion.

Notably, this money only covers through the end of 2004; thus, even more money will likely be required for later years. The $13 billion received from other countries will provide a part of the necessary funding for later years, but clearly only a small part. The cost of just maintaining U.S. troops in Iraq could cost multiple billions each year. The Congressional Budget Office, for example, estimates that even a large reduction of troops would still cost $14 billion annually. Assuming U.S. troops stay in Iraq for five years, this could amount to a whopping $70 billion, just for military costs. In addition, experts say the future costs of reconstruction and rebuilding in Iraq could top $100 billion. Thus, the total price tag for rebuilding Iraq could be over $300 billion.

Therefore, as Representative John M. Spratt Jr. says, the money put up so far "could just be the first of many installments."[48] Just exactly how much Americans will ultimately pay in addition to the $87 billion is not yet known, but President Bush has suggested that he stands ready to pay any price: "We will do what is necessary, we will spend what is necessary, to achieve this essential victory in the war on terror, to promote freedom, and to make our own nation more secure."[49]

Shouldering the cost of the war was a controversial issue among the American public.

On the one hand, some Americans felt that forking over tax dollars to be spent on the war effort was well warranted. They saw the efforts in Iraq as part of the larger war on terror and thus believed the money spent in Iraq would translate into a safer and more secure America. Many people also saw Iraq as a good investment, one that would cost money now but would yield high profits in the future. Indeed, it was hoped by many that Iraq could even-

Although Colin Powell called the October 2003 Madrid fund-raising conference a success, he admitted that the money received was short of expectations.

tually become a friendly place to do business and yield profit for a variety of American businesses.

On the other hand, the war against Iraq was undertaken during a national recession;

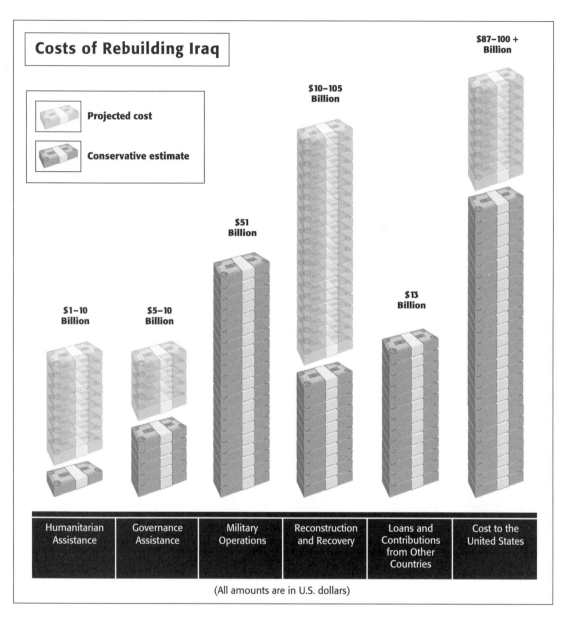

Costs of Rebuilding Iraq

Projected cost

Conservative estimate

$1–10 Billion
Humanitarian Assistance

$5–10 Billion
Governance Assistance

$51 Billion
Military Operations

$10–105 Billion
Reconstruction and Recovery

$13 Billion
Loans and Contributions from Other Countries

$87–100 + Billion
Cost to the United States

(All amounts are in U.S. dollars)

this meant that jobs, savings, and funds were scarce in different places around the United States. The U.S. government had incurred a record deficit, meaning it had spent more money than it had taken in and was in debt.

As a result of these economic conditions, many Americans struggled with layoffs, hiring freezes, and other economic challenges. Many states experienced budget shortfalls, causing numerous public programs to be trimmed or cut entirely. Therefore, many Americans, especially those who did not support the war, were disturbed that their taxes were heading abroad to fund the reconstruction of Iraq while they were lacking programs and jobs at home. How tax dollars should be spent is always a matter of debate among Americans, and talk about the looming deficit and reconstruction funding continued all through 2004.

The United States Turns to the UN

Under the pressure of such financial issues, in early 2004 the United States indicated that it might be willing to invite the United Nations to play a larger role in Iraq. U.S. officials met with Kofi Annan, UN secretary-general, to ask for the United Nations's help in matters related to the rebuilding efforts. Reaching out to the United Nations was significant because it signaled that the United States wanted to involve the international community in Iraq's future.

On January 26, 2004, agreeing to U.S. requests, Annan announced that the United Nations would send a team of elections experts to help in Iraq. Annan also said he favored eventually creating a multinational military force that would operate under the authority of the United Nations. This group ideally would help bring stability to Iraq and take some of the financial and military burden off the United States.

America's request for help marked a reversal of previous policy. At other points during the war and rebuilding, the United States had cut the United Nations out of

planning in Iraq. Now, however, it seemed willing to involve the United Nations. The United States, which was initially scorned for "going it alone" in the war effort, was now praised for its initiative in involving the international community. It was also hoped that involving the UN in Iraq's future could help bring legitimacy to a new Iraqi government. That is, it was thought that if many countries recognized and supported the Iraqi government, the Iraqi people would

U.S. Reconstruction Contracts

One of the international community's criticisms of the United States after the war was that corporations connected with the Bush administration and the U.S. military were awarded huge reconstruction contracts without giving other companies a chance to compete for them. For example, in March 2003 the Bush administration awarded a multibillion-dollar contract to repair Iraq's oil industry to Halliburton, a major U.S. contractor. The contract was criticized because Dick Cheney had run Halliburton before he became vice president. Awarding such a large job to a company with close ties to the administration was loudly criticized as favoritism.

The Halliburton issue arose again in the fall of 2003 when the company was accused of overcharging for fuel imported into Iraq. In December 2003, the Pentagon investigated these practices and concluded that the company had overcharged the U.S. government by as much as $61 million. President Bush said companies overcharging for reconstruction services would be required to repay the government, but the incident suggested that companies friendly to the administration were taking advantage of their government contacts.

accept its authority and follow new laws and rules that would be put into effect. Opening up the process to the international community may also reap large benefits for the United States: If U.S. officials permit the United Nations to become significantly involved in Iraq, other countries may be more willing to send troops and help with other reconstruction costs.

Future Military Action

Ironically, the heavy costs of the U.S. invasion and rebuilding of Iraq may prevent the United States from undertaking similar military actions against other countries in the near future. With the postwar process in Iraq proving both difficult and expensive, Americans may very well resist other military adventures and insist on diplomatic solutions instead.

Indeed, since the Iraq war, the Bush administration has already refrained from using force, responding diplomatically to WMD crises in two other countries named by Bush as part of the "axis of evil"—Iran and North Korea. Diplomacy was used despite solid evidence that both of these countries may have

already developed nuclear weapons programs, unlike Iraq, which was only suspected of trying to develop such weapons. The Bush administration's sudden conversion to diplomacy clearly reflects the experience in Iraq and the limits of U.S. military capability. The United States, quite simply, cannot afford and does not have enough troops to take on another large military or nation-building endeavor anytime in the near future. In this way, the Iraq war may have limited America's ability to respond to other WMD threats to world peace.

However, if the United States embraces diplomacy and uses the United Nations to deal with international crises, as it has in the North Korea and Iran situations, this could help to revive and strengthen the United Nations. After all, the purpose of the United Nations is to resolve world conflicts through international collaboration and collective action. One of the end results of America's war against Iraq, therefore, might be a realization that U.S. power has its limits. U.S. officials may conclude that no nation can afford—politically, militarily, or economically—to act alone to police the world.

Chapter 5

Creating a New Iraqi Government

The American plan for Iraq, from the time the war ended, was to establish an Iraqi government as soon as possible. Yet balanced against this desire was a fear that turning over power prematurely, before the Iraqis could handle the responsibilities, might lead to even greater instability, perhaps even civil war. Despite protests from Iraqis, therefore, U.S. officials at first did not grant them full sovereignty. However, faced with intensifying guerrilla attacks as well as domestic and international pressure to end America's occupation of Iraq, the transfer of power was sped up—a maneuver praised by many but one fraught with many risks.

The Challenges Posed by Iraq's Ethnic Groups

Throughout its history Iraq has been a notoriously difficult country to rule. This is mainly due to the presence of a variety of ethnic groups that do not all get along. In 1921 Britain set Iraq's boundaries in a way that grouped three very different ethnic groups—the Kurds, the Sunnis, and the Shias—into one country. Britain then established a Sunni-led government in Iraq, even though the Sunni sect was a minority of the population. These decisions inevitably led to decades of ethnic divisions and rivalries, as Sunnis discriminated against and persecuted the other two ethnic groups.

Today, the Sunnis and the Shias together make up about 75 percent of the Iraqi population. They respectively live in central and southern Iraq. Both are of Arab ancestry and are Muslim. They are divided, however, by a religious split that occurred many centuries ago. That split created the two sects—the Shias (sometimes called Shiites) and the Sunnis. The Shias form the majority in Iraq, and the Sunnis make up only about 32 percent of Iraq's population.

Despite their small numbers, the Sunnis have ruled in Iraq since its founding. They have held virtually all the power, which they used to discriminate against the Shias in terms of jobs, housing, education, and all other opportunities. The Shias were persecuted by Saddam's government (which was Sunni), and thousands were killed when they revolted against the regime in 1991. Because of this history, Shias in postwar Iraq do not trust Sunni Arabs and want to make sure that they, as a majority of the population, have a large stake in Iraq's new government. The Sunnis, meanwhile, desperately fear losing their power. They also fear that Shias who were hurt by Sunni rule will take revenge on them if given the chance to govern.

Another ethnic group persecuted by the Sunnis is the Kurds, a culturally distinct, non-Arab ethnic group living in various countries, mostly in Turkey, Iran, and Iraq. Following World War I they were promised their own country, but were never granted it. Some of these Kurds were included by the British in the country of Iraq, where they now number about 3.5 million people, or about 15 percent of the population. They are located primarily in northern Iraq.

The Kurds were treated severely by Saddam. His regime undertook ethnic cleansing campaigns during the 1970s and 1980s designed to wipe them out and take away their homes and land. For these reasons, Kurds dream of an independent Kurdish nation separate from Iraq. Ever since the 1991 Persian Gulf War, the Kurds, with U.S. military protection, have successfully governed themselves, and they seem willing to become part of a new Iraq only if they can continue to have this type of freedom within a new Iraqi government.

The very challenging mission for America in postwar Iraq, therefore, is to get the three diverse and distrustful ethnic groups to share power in a democratic government. In the past, Iraq's serious ethnic tensions were quieted only by a strong, authoritarian central government, such as Saddam's brutal dictatorship. The United States, however, wants to install not a dictatorship but a democracy, which is a sensitive and delicate undertaking in a country fraught with so many divisions.

Iraqi Self-Rule Is Delayed

Initially U.S. officials boldly predicted that a provisional Iraqi government would be created by the end of May 2003. The first U.S. administrator in Iraq, Jay Garner, for example, promised, "By the second weekend in May, you'll see the beginning of a nucleus of a temporary Iraqi government; a government with an Iraqi face on it that is totally dealing with the coalition."[50] To this end, U.S. officials organized meetings of various Iraqi factions—all three Iraqi ethnic groups (Kurds, Sunnis, and Shias) were represented. Also included were both local Iraqis and Iraqis who had been living in exile in other countries. All of these parties came together to discuss forming a provisional government for Iraq. At a meeting held on April 28, 2003, Iraqis, with U.S. encouragement, decided to hold a national conference in May to select a transitional government for Iraq. It was expected that Iraqis would quickly be granted full governing power over Iraq.

Iraqi Kurds show their support for Kurdish inclusion in Iraq's political process. Saddam's regime brutally mistreated the Kurdish people.

In mid-May, however, continuing instability, violence, and chaos in Iraq caused the United States and Britain to abruptly reverse their plans for quickly setting up a transitional government. Instead, it was announced that the coalition forces would remain in charge of Iraq for an indefinite period, assisted by a U.S.-led "interim authority," later called the Iraqi Governing Council (IGC). The IGC was not given full authority to rule Iraq but instead operated under U.S. authority and supervision. The plan was for the IGC to first write a constitution and then hold democratic elections to establish an Iraqi government that would have full power to govern. U.S. and British officials explained that the delay would allow time to include more people in the Iraqi leadership. They also said it would avoid handing over power at a time of continuing disorder, when a divided or weak government might not be able to control the country.

Iraqis were greatly disappointed—they ardently wanted to rule themselves after living for years under Saddam's dictatorship. They also feared that the delay might mean the United States wanted to maintain control over the new Iraq. Indeed, many Iraqis began to view the United States as an "occupier" rather than as a "liberator." Adel Abdel Mahdi, political adviser to one of Iraq's largest Shia political groups, for instance, openly accused the United States of going back on promises to support the rapid creation of an Iraqi-led interim government. "We were talking about an interim government, with authority to make decisions," Mahdi says, "[but the American plan is] clearly something else."[51]

Mahdi's comments reflected the disappointment felt by many other groups, including other Shia groups, Kurdish political groups, and a group of Iraqi exiles called the Iraqi National Congress. On May 25, 2003, in one of the strongest shows of dissatisfaction, an estimated ten thousand Shia Muslims marched in Baghdad, demanding that the United States immediately turn over power to an Iraqi government and withdraw its troops from the country. Several of the main Iraqi political groups submitted a formal protest to U.S. authorities.

In response to the Iraqi complaints and in an effort to better involve Iraqis in decision making, U.S. civilian administrator for Iraq L. Paul Bremer gave the IGC more power. In addition to helping to create a constitution and planning for elections, Bremer said the council could appoint Iraqi ministers who would be given control over the various departments in Iraq's government. Bremer also promised to let the council make recommendations in areas such as creating a new Iraqi currency, restarting oil production, and developing an economic strategy and education reform.

Despite these concessions, however, many Iraqis, particularly Shia leaders, continued to oppose the idea of an Iraqi council operating under American control. These protests threatened to derail the American plan for easing Iraq into full sovereignty. If influential Iraqi leaders refused to become part of the council, U.S. officials worried that its decisions would not be seen as legitimate by Iraqis or by the rest of the world. After months of difficult debate, however, U.S. fears were reduced when Iraq's main political groups agreed to join the IGC.

The Iraqi Governing Council

The twenty-five-member IGC was a diverse group made up of thirteen Shias, five Sunni Arabs, five Kurds, and two other minority representatives. Included among the newly appointed council members were exiles such as Ahmad Chalabi, head of the Iraqi National Congress; Sunni leaders such as Adnan Bajaji, part of the Independent Democrats Movement; Kurdish leaders such as Jalal Talabani, the leader of the Patriotic Union of Kurdistan; and Shia leaders such as Grand Ayatollah Ali al-Sistani, a moderate considered to be the most influential Shia in Iraq. Bremer pledged that he would "consult the Governing Council on all major decisions and questions of policy."[52] Only in exceptional circumstances, Bremer said, would the United States take action without the approval of the IGC.

By early September 2003 the council had successfully completed its first important task—naming a twenty-five-member cabinet of ministers that was expected to take over the day-to-day administration of the government from the Americans. Iraqi cabinet ministers were assigned to areas such as foreign affairs, finance, communications, internal security, and oil. The IGC also began the process of writing a new Iraqi constitution and planning for elections, steps deemed necessary by the United States before it would transfer power. The United States allowed the IGC to choose the persons who would write the constitution. American officials hoped that the process of writing a constitution and preparing for elections would allow a moderate Iraqi leader to emerge to head the first democratic Iraqi government. The United States set a December 15, 2003, deadline, for the council to act in these areas.

The process of writing a constitution and planning for elections, however, became bogged down amid deteriorating security. For example, car-bomb attacks in and around Baghdad in September 2003 made council members sometimes afraid to show up at meetings. They told U.S. administrator Bremer that they felt they had become obvious targets for assassination attempts and complained that the United States was

Iraq's Governing Council

The Iraqi Governing Council, appointed by the U.S.-led Coalition Provisional Authority (CPA) on July 13, 2003, was made up of twenty-five leaders from Iraq's various ethnic and political groups. Thirteen members of the council were Shia, five were Kurdish, five were Sunni Arabs, one was Christian, and one was Turkoman (another ethnic group in Iraq). Twenty-two members of the council were male, and three were female. Four of the council members were Iraqi exiles who had lived outside of Iraq.

Many members were already known as leaders among Iraq's ethnic groups or exile groups. The council also included a wide assortment of people from various backgrounds. Examples included a medical doctor who opposed Saddam's regime (Ayad Alawi), a Shia human rights activist (Ahmad al-Barak), an Iraqi Arab newspaper publisher (Saad al-Bazzaz), a woman and leader of the Iraqi Women's Organization (Sondul Chapouk), a female foreign affairs expert (Akila al-Hashemi), a female head of a maternity hospital in Iraq (Raja Habib al-Khuzaai), and a Sunni Muslim who once served as Iraqi foreign minister and ambassador to the United Nations (Adnan Pachachi).

The council was not awarded full sovereignty; it was required to work with the CPA on all areas of policy and budgets. It was, however, charged with appointing new Iraqi cabinet ministers and with establishing procedures for writing a new constitution. It was also given the power to decide how it wanted to organize itself. The council chose to make the position of president of the council a rotating one in which nine council members would share time as president, with each member serving as president for one month at a time.

not providing them with adequate security. These warnings proved prophetic when one council member, Akila al-Hashemi, was gunned down and killed on the street on September 20, 2003.

Iraqis Demand More Power

Council members became increasingly frustrated with the degree of American control. In September 2003, several prominent IGC leaders demanded that U.S. authorities transfer the day-to-day security duties from American troops to Iraqi militia forces. These forces, they claimed, could work with local civic and tribal leaders to tailor security strategies to each part of the country and in this way be more effective than the Americans.

Newly appointed Iraqi cabinet ministers joined council members in criticizing the American occupation and the centralized power exercised by Administrator Bremer and the U.S. military commander in Iraq, Lieutenant General Ricardo Sanchez. They demanded that they be given more power over Iraqi concerns. As Hayder Awad Aabadi, Iraq's new minister of communications, explains, "Iraqis are a very proud people. They will not be motivated in a situation where things are run by a foreign occupying power."[53]

Next, Iraqi Shias demanded that commission members be democratically elected

Akila al-Hashemi, an American-appointed member of the Iraqi Governing Council, was assassinated in 2003.

rather than appointed by the United States. On June 30 Iraq's leading moderate Shia cleric, Grand Ayatollah Ali al-Sistani, issued a "fatwa," or religious ruling, rejecting the idea of an American-controlled constitutional commission. He also asserted that Iraqis should elect the drafters of their constitution.

Shias, the majority in Iraq, favor democratic elections for these matters because they believe they would likely win such elections and gain control of the government in Iraq.

Squabbles and disagreements ensued over the drafting of the Iraqi constitution. Shias, Sunnis, and Kurds all mistrusted each other, and each feared that the other groups would try to dominate the drafting process. Ultimately, prominent members of the council rejected the U.S. assignment of writing a constitution prior to self-rule. Such a task, they said, was too divisive at this point in Iraq's recovery. Also, writing a constitution and holding elections could take a year or more—too long for Iraqis to remain under the control of the Americans. Instead, the Iraqi leaders declared that they wanted to immediately assume the powers of a provisional government and write the constitution later. The group planned to write a basic civil law that would be used to govern Iraq temporarily.

With this rebellion by the IGC, members brought the issue of Iraqi sovereignty full circle, back to the point when Iraqis first opposed the U.S. delay of self-rule. As Adel Abdel Mahdi, a representative of the Supreme Council for the Islamic Revolution in Iraq, puts it, "We are returning back to May. . . . At that time, the Americans said no [to immediate Iraqi self-rule], but now they are more willing to listen."[54]

A New Plan for Iraqi Self-Governance

As division and ineffectiveness plagued the IGC, U.S. officials became increasingly disenchanted with council members. In addition to the policy differences, American officials complained that the council was moving too slowly on important issues and failing to communicate with ordinary Iraqis. Also, they lamented that the council was meeting

Islamic Values

Creating a sovereign government in Iraq has raised the question, Will the government be run by Islamic religious leaders and will it embrace Islamic values? Even defining Islamic values is difficult, because Muslims differ among themselves about the true meaning of Islam. What both conservative and liberal Muslims seem to share is a belief that Western values—often defined by Muslims as materialistic, amoral, and antireligious—should not corrupt the religious morality of Arab cultures.

Yet to Westerners, Islamic values have often been seen as unenlightened, particularly regarding the treatment of women. Islamic views of sexual modesty, for instance, often require women to cover their bodies in public and for men and women to be segregated in public places. In some cases, these requirements have prevented women from having careers or becoming active in public affairs. However, Muslim women have always had the right to own property independent of their husbands and receive inheritances—rights not granted in Western societies until much later.

Because of the varying interpretations, many observers fear that Islamic values could be interpreted by a new Iraqi government to discriminate against women and non-Muslim minorities. In addition, it is feared that an Islamic-influenced government might enforce religious laws in ways that would punish non-Muslims for behavior that is considered sinful in Islam. The role of Islam in Iraq's new government remains to be seen.

only three times a week and often without key members who were busy, traveling abroad, or too worried about their personal safety to attend the sessions. Indeed, three months after its appointment by the United States, the IGC had developed a reputation among U.S. staff as well as many Iraqis as a largely ineffective body weakened by internal divisions and politics.

As a result of dissatisfaction with the council and concern about its inability to move forward with writing a constitution, in November 2003 the United States offered a new plan—to allow Iraqis to create a new transitional Iraqi government by June 2004. This transitional government would be given full authority to govern the country until a constitution could be written and elections could be held. Part of the deal was that U.S. military forces would remain in Iraq to maintain security. The United States hoped, by hastening the transfer of power, the new plan would end Iraqis' resentment of the United States as an occupying power and help reduce the attacks on U.S. soldiers and other targets. Administrator Bremer promised to hold discussions with the IGC to further develop the new process.

The U.S. announcement created a firm date for giving Iraqis the sovereignty they had been seeking. Although the risk of turning over power too early still remained, the United States gained many side benefits. For example, turning over political authority to the Iraqis would silence much of the international and domestic criticism of President Bush's Iraq policy (since critics had asked for

a quicker transfer of power). In addition, the new timetable offered the United States a convenient "exit strategy"—a first step toward getting the United States out of Iraq. Although some U.S. troops would remain, the United States would no longer be making the decisions about Iraq's political and economic development.

The Shias Demand Democracy

The IGC approved the new U.S. plan and timetable and agreed to dissolve the council once the new provisional government was created in June 2004. Under the U.S. proposal, caucuses (or meetings) would be held in each of Iraq's eighteen provinces to appoint a transitional legislative body made up of several hundred Iraqis from various regions and social sectors. This legislature, in turn, would choose a prime minister and a provisional government by June 30, 2004. The provisional government would then be given responsibility for drafting Iraq's constitution.

Soon, however, the plan encountered a major obstacle when Grand Ayatollah Ali al-Sistani, the prominent Shia leader in Iraq, publicly announced his opposition to the method the Americans proposed for choosing the new government. Ayatollah al-Sistani rejected the caucus-style process and insisted that the June elections be direct democratic elections. That is, instead of having the caucuses elect Iraqi leaders, al-Sistani believed each and every Iraqi should be allowed to cast a vote. As al-Sistani said in a written statement, "We see no alternative but to go back

to the people for choosing their representatives."[55] Iraqi Shias quickly showed their support for al-Sistani's demands for democracy; thousands turned out to protest the American plan in cities throughout Iraq.

Al-Sistani's objections placed American officials in a tricky position: It was difficult for the United States to oppose al-Sistani's call

A vendor cleans a poster picturing Ayatollah Ali al-Sistani (right). The ayatollah encouraged Shia Muslims to reject the U.S. plan for Iraq's government.

for popular democracy because this was what U.S. officials said they wanted to bring to Iraq. However, U.S. officials were concerned that a direct election could not be held immediately in Iraq because there was no reliable list of eligible voters. Such a list would take time to develop, but American officials did not want to further postpone elections. Shia leaders suggested that Iraq's food-rations registry be used as a voter list. Yet this idea also had its problems. Many families were deleted from the list by Saddam if, for example, a family member deserted from the army. Yet another idea proposed by other Iraqi leaders was for power to be transferred from the U.S. to an expanded version of the IGC, so that elections could be held in 2004 to elect the provisional government. This proposal, however, also had its drawback: U.S. officials worried that since the IGC members were chosen by the United States, it would not be viewed as legitimate by the Iraqi people.

Faced with these dilemmas, the United States, together with Iraqi leaders from the IGC, appealed to the United Nations for help. U.S. officials hoped the United Nations could resolve the question of how to elect an Iraqi government, perhaps by helping to organize elections and certifying their legitimacy. UN secretary-general Kofi Annan agreed to send UN elections experts to Iraq, but as of January 2004 the outcome of al-Sistani's press for direct elections was unclear. What was clear, however, was that the Shias have enormous power in postwar Iraq, and that they intend to ensure they are fairly represented in any new Iraqi government. As al-Sistani supporter Ahmad Hadi says, "Our future, our fate lies in elections, not in appointing a government that doesn't rep-

resent the people. We are just asking for free elections, for real democracy."[56]

Ethnic Divisions Emerge

After the Shias made clear their preference for elections, Sunni and Kurdish politicians also began making their own demands. Coalition officials feared that conflicting demands from the three groups could divide Iraq according to ethnic lines and, even worse, spark a civil or religious war.

The Kurds, for instance, bowing to American pressure, refrained from declaring themselves a separate, independent nation, as they have always dreamed of doing. Instead, they agreed to become part of the new Iraq. However, they insisted that the new constitution guarantee that they will never again be persecuted by the government. They are willing to have a central government handle foreign policy, money policy, and national defense, but they want the power to govern themselves as a separate region within Iraq—a system known as a federation. In addition, Kurdish politicians want to keep their own security forces, called *pesh merga,* and retain control of Kirkuk, a northern city known for its vast oil resources.

The Sunnis also began asserting themselves. Concerned that they were being pushed aside by the Shia demands for power, in January 2004 Sunni leaders formed the State Council for the Sunnis to present a unified political voice for Sunnis. The Sunni council is made up largely of Sunni clerics and has 160 members, including representatives from the two Sunni Islamic parties on the Iraqi Governing Council. The Sunni council denies that it is linked in any way to Sunni followers of Saddam who are behind the insurgency in Iraq, but, like the insurgents, it wants an end to the U.S. occupation and a voice in any new Iraqi government.

An Islamic Government in Iraq

The other critical issue to be considered in any future Iraqi government is religion. Because Shias form the majority of the population, truly democratic elections will likely result in a Shia-led or Shia-controlled government. However, most Shias do not believe religion and politics should be kept separate, as they are in secular countries such as the United States. Shias have made it clear that they want Islamic principles to be respected in Iraq's new constitution and government. Ayatollah al-Sistani, for example, has stated that the constitution should guarantee individual liberties, but only as long as they are consistent "with the religious facts and the social values of the Iraqi people."[57] What these broad guidelines would mean in practice, however, is yet to be determined.

A Shia government, U.S. officials fear, might turn into a fundamentalist Islamic government—that is, a government run by Islamic religious leaders who would impose Islamic religious values on everyone in Iraq. Such a government would be similar to the repressive Islamic government in Iran and might become anti-American in much the same way Iran has. This type of Islamic government might also threaten the rights of

Many Iraqis resent American involvement in their affairs and feel the same anti-American sentiment as these Palestinians.

the Kurds and the Sunnis, who do not adhere to the laws and beliefs of Shia Islam. This scenario could be highly divisive and lead to even greater instability in Iraq, perhaps even to civil war.

However, it is also possible that a Shia government might not necessarily be harmful to American interests—in fact, American fears of an Iranian-style Islamic government coming to power in Iraq might be misplaced.

Grand Ayatollah Ali al-Sistani

Grand Ayatollah Ali al-Sistani, seventy-three years old, is the most important Islamic religious leader from the Shia ethnic group in Iraq. Al-Sistani was born near the Iranian city of Mashhad, a holy site for Muslims. As a child and young man, al-Sistani studied the Koran, the Muslim holy book. In 1952 he moved to the Iraqi city of Najaf, where he studied with the several leading Shia clerics. In 1992 al-Sistani was selected to head an important group of religious schools in Najaf. Since then, he has written books on Islamic law and developed a reputation as one of the top Shia religious leaders in the world.

Al-Sistani is considered a moderate, and he supported the U.S. occupation of Iraq. However, he has insisted that Iraq's interim government and the drafters of Iraq's new constitution be selected through direct elections. He also wants Iraq's constitution to respect Islamic law by upholding conservative Islamic religious values. One of al-Sistani's main rivals for Islamic leadership in Iraq was Mohammed Baqir al-Sadr, who was shot and killed by Saddam's forces in 1999. Since then, al-Sistani has emerged as Iraq's most influential Islamic leader. He was appointed to the interim Iraqi Governing Council by the United States and is expected to play a major role in Iraq's next government.

Although Shias form a majority in Iraq, they are not all controlled by Iran's Islamic leaders and do not uniformly agree that Iraq's government should be run by Islamic religious leaders. Many Shias want to see a secular, nonreligious government that respects religious freedom and minority rights.

Indeed, as the majority group in Iraq, Shias have a strong stake in keeping the country stable and unified, and the only way to do that is for the government to respect the rights and aspirations of other groups. Shias, therefore, may not institute an Islamic government that is insensitive to the rights and aspirations of other Iraqis. As one expert on Islamic law, Noah Feldman, says, "It's going to be tricky and it's delicate, but it's going to be solvable, because in the end the Shia clerics are open to a state that's a democratic state but is also respectful of Islam."[58]

Grand Ayatollah al-Sistani's followers and other Shia leaders have echoed this view. Sheik Saghir, one of the Shia clerics on the council's constitutional committee, asserts, "We don't want Islamic government in Iraq—it would be a loss for Islam."[59] Similarly, Abdul Aziz al-Hakim, an Islamic clergyman and council member who is close to al-Sistani, states, "We don't want at this point to have an Islamic government. We don't want a Shia government. We want a broad-based, democratic government."[60]

The United States may have to support whatever kind of government emerges in Iraq, religious or secular. Having agreed to transfer power quickly, the United States cannot now easily withdraw that promise. Also, without appearing to be hypocritical, U.S. officials cannot challenge the Shia call for truly democratic elections or some reasonable alternative.

Once an interim Iraqi government is elected, the United States will have little control over it or how it decides to draft Iraq's new constitution. Therefore, it will be Shia, Sunni, and Kurdish delegates, not U.S. policy makers, who will have to balance the conservative Shia and Islamic values with the more liberal values of most Sunnis and Kurds. This process will ultimately determine the important questions in Iraq—questions such as the rights of women, the rights of religious and ethnic minorities, how closely the Iraqi constitution will follow Islamic law, and whether Islamic clerics will be appointed as judges and given authority to overrule laws passed by the elected legislature.

Many observers see this process as a healthy sign of democracy in Iraq. As Brandeis University professor Yitzhak Nakash explains, "What we are witnessing is a very healthy bargaining session over what will be the relationship between religion and politics in Iraq and over the process of choosing legitimate national and communal leaders."[61] *New York Times* columnist Thomas L. Friedman argues that America should respect and encourage this process: "We must not try to abort this unfolding discussion among Iraqis. In fact, we should be proud of it. We are fostering a much-needed free political dialogue in the heart of the Arab world. . . . There is no more important political project for the U.S. in the world today."[62]

An Interim Constitution

In taking first steps toward the process of self-government, Iraq's leaders finally endorsed an interim constitution on March 8, 2004. The signing of the constitution had been delayed several times by political deadlock and by terrorist attacks, but all twenty-five members of the Iraqi Governing Council signed the document and agreed to its provisions. Although certain Shia leaders took issue with parts of the temporary constitution, they nevertheless signed the document, saying that it was in the best interests of the country to do so. The adoption of the interim constitution marked a milestone in the attempt to implement democracy in the new Iraq. States one council member, Adnan Pachachi, "This is a great and historic day. . . . We have produced a law that we can be justly proud of."[63]

The interim constitution resembles the U.S. Constitution in certain ways. For example, it features a bill of rights that includes the right to freedom of speech, assembly, and religion. It provides civilian control over the military and adopts a system of checks and balances to ensure that no one branch of government will usurp power from another. It also provides guarantees for women's rights.

The temporary constitution is also uniquely Iraqi, however. For example, it declares Islam as Iraq's official religion and makes a point of saying Islam will be used as a source of legislation. It also makes a special attempt to recognize Kurdish identity and declares Kurdish as one of the official languages of the new Iraq. This reference to the Kurds is important considering their history of persecution in the country. As Kurdish leader and council member Massoud Barzani proclaimed at the signing ceremonies, "This is the first time that we Kurds feel that we are citizens of Iraq."[64]

The interim constitution was signed nearly a year after Saddam Hussein was toppled from power. Despite the progress that it marks, however, Iraq continues to be a shaky nation with an uncertain future. Symbolizing this instability was the scene beyond the walls of the signing ceremony. As Iraqi leaders met, guerrillas fired mortars at a Baghdad police station, wounding two policemen and three civilians. In the city of Mosul, insurgents opened fire on a car carrying two city council members, killing one and wounding the other. These attacks make clear that while progress is being made, Iraq's path to democracy is still quite treacherous.

☆ Chapter 6 ☆

Reconstruction Efforts

Reconstruction in Iraq began almost as soon as the war ended. The United States soon discovered that rebuilding Iraq would take longer, be more involved, and cost much more than first expected. Even before the war, Iraq was a broken country, and the chaos of the war and its aftermath made a quick recovery even more difficult. With American efforts, international aid, and Iraqi expertise, however, it was hoped that a new Iraq would be built step by step.

An Already-Damaged Infrastructure

U.S. forces quickly realized that Iraq's infrastructure was in much worse condition than anyone had suspected. Saddam, throughout his three-decade rule, had simply failed to fund repairs and maintenance for basic utilities, roads, and public buildings. As Nesreen M. Siddeek Berwari, the Iraqi minister of municipalities and public works, explains, "We cannot talk about [reconstruction] without revisiting the history and the heritage that we took over, which was three decades of total neglect of public service."[65] Throughout Saddam's rule, Iraqis had managed to keep services going only by masterly and ingenious tinkering and engineering.

As a result, most of Iraq's electrical, water, and telephone systems were barely functioning, if at all. Even before the war electrical power was not always available in much of the country. Sewage systems in many neighborhoods were frequently backed up, and wastewater was dumped directly into major rivers without being treated for toxic pollutants. These systems required major repairs, substantially increasing reconstruction costs and making early progress in Iraq appear to be achingly slow.

The slow pace of reconstruction, in turn, led to international criticism of U.S. rebuilding efforts as well as open frustration among Iraqis. Complaints were voiced by Iraqis who had expected the United States to quickly fix the almost thirty years' worth

An Iraqi woman collects contaminated water. Providing the Iraqi people with a supply of clean water was one of the chief aims of U.S. reconstruction efforts.

of problems plaguing their nation. These critics were particularly vocal throughout the summer of 2003, when temperatures in Iraq reached well above one hundred degrees Fahrenheit and they had to live in the sweltering heat without the benefit of reliable electricity or air conditioning.

Looting and Sabotage

Yet another factor that inhibited reconstruction efforts was the damage caused by massive looting at the end of the war. By August 2003, for example, looters had stolen much of the copper wire and steel from some 635 electrical towers that carried the main lines for Iraq's power distribution grid. In addition, looters took the computerized parts that were essential for preventing disastrous electrical overloads. Much of Iraq's already crumbling infrastructure was thus stripped down during the postwar period.

As work began to repair the twofold damage caused by neglect and looting, U.S. military forces and contractors found their progress further crippled by guerrilla sabotage attacks. The work done on newly repaired utilities and oil pipelines was quickly undone when insurgents bombed or otherwise attacked them in the hopes of derailing the U.S. occupation. For example, an important oil pipeline in northern Iraq was repeatedly bombed, preventing vital oil sales that U.S. officials hoped would help pay for the country's rebuilding.

In addition, the lack of security and dangerous working conditions, particularly around Baghdad and the central part of Iraq, delayed and sometimes completely halted reconstruction and relief work. Construction and aid workers were attacked and sometimes killed by insurgents who shot at them or planted bombs—again in an effort to end the U.S. occupation and rebuilding effort. Contractors were forced to hire extra police to protect workers and to increase pay, further adding to reconstruction costs.

The deteriorating security conditions also made it difficult to convince experienced Western contractors to come to Iraq to do the reconstruction work. Multiple terrorist attacks on private contractors and their employees, as well as relief agencies, caused an exodus of relief groups and contractors from the country. The United Nations, the

Red Cross, and organizations such as Save the Children and Doctors Without Borders evacuated most of their staffs from Baghdad.

However, by the end of 2003 significant work was being done that was expected to produce visible results for the Iraqi population. As Tom Wheelock, director of Iraq's infrastructure programs for the U.S. Agency for International Development (USAID), said in November 2003, "There's a lot going on. . . . We're on the cusp of [improving] people's quality of life." [66] One soldier, Art Messer, shared his thoughts about the reconstruction progress in Iraq:

> The towns I saw a month ago with raw sewage running in the streets and between the buildings are now showing marked signs of improvement! I went through some towns a few days ago and the sewage was drained away and drying up. I saw new construction and building upgrades everywhere! I saw power lines being repaired and new utility lines being installed everywhere. I saw many Iraqis working and living and getting back to a normal life. [67]

The progress was concentrated largely in the southern and northern parts of Iraq, where the security was better and the working conditions were safer. These areas, populated mostly by Kurds (in the north) and Shias (in the south) welcomed the American reconstruction effort. In and around Baghdad, however, where the Iraqi guerrilla activity was concentrated, reconstruction projects slowed considerably. In strongholds of the insurgency, such as Ramadi and Fallujah, relief activity virtually stopped. Yet even in Baghdad, some improvements were made. Streets were cleaned of most of the debris and garbage that had built up during the war, and power was restored to much of the city, although both homes and businesses were still plagued by electrical blackouts.

Restoring Electricity

The first priority for reconstructing Iraq was to repair its infrastructure—a large part of this was getting electricity turned on for Iraqis. Engineers with the U.S. Army Corps, USAID, Bechtel (an American company that was awarded the first main reconstruction contract), and the new Iraqi ministries worked together on these repairs. Because the problems in Iraq were more serious than first anticipated, the initial work focused on

A soldier guards an Iraqi power plant. Army engineers worked with the new Iraqi ministries and Bechtel, an engineering company, to restore power in postwar Iraq.

emergency repairs to electrical lines and other public works rather than on major reconstruction. Bechtel hoped to undertake more comprehensive electrical rebuilding projects in the future, when more money became available.

To reestablish electrical power, contractors installed new electricity generators in large power plants and other sites such as hospitals, clinics, and oil refineries. They purchased the materials needed to restart boilers at the plants and started on other needed repairs. They also began construction on a system of electrical lines from power plants in southern Iraq to Baghdad, where the most power was needed. As soon as April 2003, some power had been restored to many parts of Baghdad, but other areas still had none. The power shortage lasted well into the hot summer of 2003, but by that fall electricity was generally and regularly available, at least intermittently, in Baghdad, Basra, and parts of southern Iraq. By November one of two planned southern electrical lines was operational, and Iraq was producing almost 4,400 megawatts—as much power as it did before the war. Bechtel predicted Iraq would be producing an additional 440 megawatts by the summer of 2004 and by the end of 2004 it would have some 4,000 megawatts of additional electricity.

Water, Communications, and Transportation

Improvements to Iraq's water purification and sewage treatment facilities were also vi-tally important, as clean drinking water is essential to keep people from becoming ill. Because of their dilapidated state, the job of repairing these systems was perhaps even more daunting than fixing Iraq's electrical grid. In Baghdad, for instance, each day 200 million gallons of wastewater were simply poured into the nearby Tigris River without being treated to remove dangerous pollutants and bacteria, which can cause disease. This untreated, bacteria-laden water then was used downstream as the source of drinking water for the entire city of Basra. To fix this dangerously unhealthy situation, contractors renovated Baghdad's sewage treatment plants, dredged the water reservoirs in Basra, and also repaired that city's water purification plant. These projects were expected to significantly improve Iraq's sanitation by the end of 2003.

Communications systems also needed repair. Iraq's telephone network, which once served approximately 1.2 million people, was seriously damaged by the war, disrupting the country's telephone service. In Baghdad, for example, twelve out of thirty-eight telephone exchange switches were destroyed, leaving 240,000 telephone lines (or almost half of the city) without service. U.S. contractors therefore began work to restore the backbone of the system—a fiber-optic cable that runs from Baghdad in the north to Basra in the south—and to repair the telephone switching system in Baghdad. An international satellite gateway system also will be installed to allow Iraqis to make international calls.

In addition, in October 2003 Iraq's Ministry of Telecommunications awarded three licenses to bring commercial mobile phone service to Iraq. Unlike many of the other reconstruction projects that were awarded to U.S. companies, these licenses were granted to a group of Arab companies—Egypt's Orascom Telecom, Mobile Telecommunications Company of Kuwait, and Wataniya Telecom, also from Kuwait. At least two Iraqi companies, Dijla Telecommunications Corporation and Asia Cell, are also involved. Iraq's mobile telephone service was expected to begin in 2004.

Work also began on repairing roads, bridges, airports, public buildings, and waterways. U.S. military engineers were sent to the port of Umm Qasr, in southeastern Iraq, to dredge and remove silt that had accumulated and make the port deep enough to accommodate large ships. Grain and other humanitarian aid items could then be brought into Iraq via ships that use the port. U.S. and Iraqi officials also repaired the two main Iraqi airports. Baghdad International Airport and a smaller one in Basra were quickly restored to their 1991 pre–Gulf War operational status and were expected to open to commercial traffic as soon as this was considered safe. (Continuing missile attacks on helicopters and other aircraft made flying Iraqi skies quite treacherous.) Plans were also drawn up to rebuild bridges and roads to increase transportation around the country.

Restarting Oil Production

Another important priority for the U.S.-led coalition was restoring Iraq's oil production.

U.S. officials hoped that oil revenues, which are Iraq's main source of income and its main export, would help pay for the high costs of reconstruction. Thanks to the efforts of Halliburton, the U.S. company given a contract for Iraqi oil repairs, and the work of talented Iraqi oil engineers and technicians, oil began flowing from some of Iraq's oilfields in May 2003. On June 22, Iraq exported its first oil since the war. Regular oil exports, however, were delayed because of severe looting and sabotage of oil facilities during the months following the war. Yet by the fall of 2003 oil production was ahead of schedule; in 2004 Iraq is expected to produce over 2 million barrels per day, the same amount it produced before the war. This will provide $20 billion per year in income to Iraq.

The cost of repairs to the oil facilities was sharply higher than initial estimates. U.S. authorities at first predicted that critical repairs would cost about $1.1 billion, but in October 2003 the Bush administration asked the U.S. Congress for an additional $2.1 billion for rebuilding the oil industry. Much of the money was spent to make the same repairs repeatedly, as a result of sabotage. Often a pipeline blown up by guerrillas would be fixed, then blown up again days later. Also, more than $3 million was spent to import oil from other countries to cover the shortages of gasoline and cooking gas in Iraq.

Given the continuing problems with security, it was unclear when Iraq would be able to further increase oil production or what additional funds might be required. Experts say that although the United States spent

The Iraqi Symphony Visits America

As part of an effort to show the world the benefits of a free Iraq, U.S. officials arranged for Iraq's National Symphony Orchestra to perform at the Kennedy Center in Washington, D.C., on December 9, 2003. President Bush and other dignitaries attended the event, which was meant to generate support for Iraq's cultural institutions. In Phillip Kurata's article "Iraq National Symphony Performs in Washington," U.S. secretary of state Colin Powell explains the significance of the visit: "The Iraqi National Symphony testifies to the power of the arts, the power of the arts to keep hope alive, even under the cruelest oppressor. The American people can be proud that they will be here and that we are helping the men and women of Iraq realize their long-held dream of freedom."

The sixty-three-member Iraqi symphony was founded in 1959. It is made up of Shias, Sunnis, Kurds, and members of other ethnic groups, and it includes four women. The orchestra features traditional Arab musical instruments, such as the *balaban,* the *daf,* the *santur,* the *tar,* the *oud,* and the *zarib.*

U.S. conductor Leonard Slatkin (left) and Iraqi conductor Mohammed Ezzat return to the stage for a curtain call after the Kennedy Center concert.

hundreds of millions of dollars to repair the oil pipes and pumps above ground, it ignored even more serious problems with Iraq's underground oil reservoirs, which could severely limit the amount of oil Iraq can produce in the future. For example, the Kirkuk oil field in northern Iraq reportedly suffers from too much water seeping into its oil deposits, a problem that could reduce its productivity in the long run. However, American officials needed immediate oil revenues to help pay for reconstruction, and they were

reluctant to undertake major efforts to improve conditions beyond what they were before the war.

Foreign investments in the oil industry might help solve Iraq's long-term oil development problems. Given the current security problems, it likely will be several years

A soldier secures the area as smoke billows from the Basra pipeline. Sabotage of pipelines throughout Iraq has hindered efforts to restore the country's oil production.

before any foreign oil company will consider investing in Iraq. Yet many observers say that Iraq is still highly attractive to oil executives looking for new oil fields. Iraq contains some of the biggest oil reserves in the world, and if some of the current security problems are resolved, Iraq may be a far more peaceful place to do business than many other more volatile oil sites around the world. As of the end of 2003, however, the continuing sabotage on oil pipelines made most investors wary and imposed oil shortages that even in December 2003 forced Iraqis to wait up to half a day to fill their cars with gasoline.

Resuming Normal Life

Although parts of Iraq remained dangerous for ordinary Iraqis, some aspects of normal life resumed. For example, by the end of 2003 most Iraqis had ample food, basic health care services, and some access to basic utilities. Coalition forces continued food-ration programs begun by Saddam after international sanctions were imposed on Iraq in 1990. The program delivers a basket of rations (rice, flour, beans, sugar, oil, salt, powdered milk, tea, soap, and laundry detergent) every month to every citizen, rich or poor. Many affluent Iraqis accept the rations and then sell the food for cash.

American authorities believe a market system would provide food more cheaply and efficiently than a government-run system, however. They eventually want to find a way to end the program without having people go hungry. One idea was to replace the rations with cash payments or some version of food stamps and limit the payments only to the needy. However, many Iraqis fear that they will not be able to afford food if the rations program is stopped. If the price for food increases, their stamps or cash will be worth less. The key to any transition, therefore, will be enacting measures that will prevent food prices from skyrocketing.

Another priority for U.S. authorities was sending Iraqi children back to school—a huge step toward returning normalcy to the country. Accordingly, approximately 1,595 schools (or about one-fifth of Iraq's schools) were renovated, many supplied with new desks and books. Students returned to schools on October 1, 2003, even though some schools were still damaged and lacked adequate textbooks and supplies.

Returning students faced significant changes in their curricula and school routines. They no longer see a portrait of Saddam in their classrooms, and they do not start the day with chants praising him as they used to. Also, under Saddam's rule virtually every subject in school, including math and science, was permeated with state-required pictures and stories that glorified Saddam. As Nada al-Jalili, an elementary school teacher at the Tigris School for Girls in Baghdad, explains, "We had to include [Saddam] in every lesson plan or we'd be in trouble with the Baath Party. . . . Whenever his name was mentioned, it had be followed with 'God protect him and keep him our president.'"[68] New textbooks were therefore printed to remove all such references to Saddam and the Baath Party.

Women in Iraq

Recent events in Iraq have made life difficult for the nation's women, but it has not always been that way. Iraqi women who grew up during the 1950s, 1960s, and 1970s enjoyed a good deal of freedom and choice. This earlier generation of women had greater access to education, were active in the workforce, and could live independently. Women at that time were involved in politics and government and worked as lawyers, judges, and government ministers.

Things changed, however, during the 1980s and the 1990s, after Saddam Hussein took over. Saddam's regime used sexual violence against women to recruit them for political service; for example, it is reported that women were raped, the rape was videotaped, and the women were then blackmailed into spying for the government. In addition, Saddam's followers sexually harassed women for their own sexual pleasure. If a member of the regime saw a women to whom he was attracted in a public restaurant or at a university, he felt entitled to have sex with her, regardless of her feelings or whether she was married. The United Nations' economic sanctions during the 1990s also contributed to a deterioration of women's rights. Salaries dropped, education was less available, and many women chose to stay home rather than go out to work in the frightening atmosphere created by Saddam and his followers.

In postwar Iraq, therefore, safety and security are huge issues for women. Mostly, Iraqi women simply want an end to their suffering. For this reason, they want to be involved in Iraq's reconstruction and government process, to make sure that women have a voice in the new Iraq.

U.S. protection since 1991, recovered quickly from the war and experienced little of the violence that plagued the rest of Iraq. Satellite television is available, people work and go to school, and at night, both women and men go out to restaurants, tea shops, and Internet salons.

In Baghdad, when curfews were lifted in late October 2003, Iraqis poured into the streets to shop and socialize. Coffeehouses were packed, and restaurants began to serve families for the first time since the beginning of the war. Indeed, even women and girls, once fearful of appearing in public because they were often targeted by criminals, began venturing onto the streets and into restaurants. Iraqis, free to travel for the first time since 1991, also began booking vacations to the more peaceful parts of Iraq and to neighboring countries. In addition, banks opened and found customers eager to open accounts, something many Iraqis would not have done under Saddam's regime due to the widespread corruption among government and bank officials.

Because of the continuing bomb attacks, however, many people continued to feel afraid. As Rana al-Bidhani, a twenty-two-year-old student, puts it, "Life is getting back to normal; we are adapting to the situation, but we are still afraid of bombs." [69]

Creating Jobs and Income

Perhaps the most critical challenge that U.S. officials in Iraq faced was providing jobs. The war and postwar chaos all but destroyed business activity in Iraq. In addition, U.S.

Other social activities were also slowly being resumed in parts of Iraq despite the continuing security problems. Northern Iraq, in particular, where Kurds enjoyed independence and economic growth under administrators disbanded the country's largest employer—the government. About half a million people who used to work for Iraq's armed forces, government ministries, state-owned businesses, and military and weapons companies promptly lost their jobs when the U.S. defeated Saddam's regime.

On June 2, 2003, U.S. administrator L. Paul Bremer announced a $70-million temporary jobs program that would pay Iraqis low wages to collect trash and rebuild schools. In addition, the Iraqi Governing Council, with U.S. permission, began making payments to about two hundred thousand military officers. They also paid full salaries to approximately 1.3 million employees of government ministries and government-owned

companies, even though there was no work for them to do. U.S. officials did this to provide these workers with enough cash to survive and to encourage the circulation of cash in Iraq's broken economy.

The United States and its allies also trained and armed more than fifty thousand Iraqis for a new police force, civil defense force, and army. By the fall of 2003, in fact, Iraqi police were already in place in many areas of Iraq. A five-hundred-person Iraqi police force had begun to patrol in Basra,

Under Saddam Hussein, Iraqi teachers earned subsistence wages. Today, as a result of U.S. reconstruction efforts, teachers are paid enough to live comfortably.

and most of Iraq's other eighty-nine cities began setting up their own police forces. Another thirty-five thousand Iraqis were to be trained over a two-year period in Jordan, where they would receive eight weeks of basic training. The U.S. also set up police academies inside Iraq. Plans were made to train forty thousand troops for a new Iraqi army—which U.S. officials hoped would be in the field by 2004—as well as a new civil defense force, or militia, which would help U.S. soldiers search for Iraqi insurgents. By December 2003 U.S. forces had already trained five thousand Iraqi militiamen, who were working under U.S. command and patrolling with U.S. and British troops.

Despite these emergency jobs measures, however, at least one-third of Iraqis remained unemployed as of the end of 2003. Also, a Fall 2003 report by the United Nations and the World Food Program claimed that almost half of Iraq's 26.3 million citizens remain poor and in need of assistance. Jobs and income for many Iraqis, therefore, depend on long-term economic growth.

For those lucky enough to get jobs paid for by reconstruction dollars—such as policemen, teachers, and construction workers—earnings have increased greatly compared to prewar standards. Before the war, for example, Kifah Karim, a teacher at a Baghdad primary school, earned together with her husband only $19 per month; now they earn close to $450 each month. As described by the *Economist*, "[The Karims] buy 2–3 kilos of meat a week, and have recently purchased a new fridge, a television, a TV satellite dish, a VCR and a CD player."[70] Indeed, for those able to buy them, once-scarce goods are now readily available. Used cars, for instance, have flooded into Iraq; some estimates say as many as 250,000 cars have been imported into Iraq since the war's end. Satellite dishes, once banned by Saddam to keep Iraqis isolated, are another hot consumer item. As shopper Luay Hasoon explains, "We were deprived of many things before. Now it's up to one's mind whether to buy something or not. It's a civilized thing."[71]

Rebuilding Iraq's Economy

These products and services were not immediately available to Iraqis after the war ended. First, the United States had to persuade the United Nations to remove economic sanctions that had hampered the Iraqi economy for almost thirteen years following the Persian Gulf War. Sanctions had barred seemingly simple items, such as candles, light bulbs, aluminum foil, and batteries. Without allowing such everyday items, it seemed the Iraqi reconstruction project would never get off the ground. Soon after the war's end, therefore, the United States went to the United Nations and negotiated an end to sanctions. Iraq was free to resume imports and exports without any type of international restriction. This new freedom was essential to allow Iraq to begin selling its oil to other countries and to produce income to help fund Iraq's reconstruction. It also encouraged Iraqi companies to export their products and foreign companies to send goods to Iraq.

U.S. officials next set up an international trade system through the Central Bank of Iraq and a group of private banks. Under this system, Iraqi banks could open credit lines to help Iraqis pay for goods needed by Iraqi ministries, government-owned factories, and private companies. The various Iraqi ministries, for example, desperately needed everything from oil field technology to transport services and telecommunications equipment. U.S. administrator Bremer said this trade credit system would be a symbol to the world that Iraq was once again open for business.

Other efforts to rebuild Iraq's economy soon followed. U.S. officials, for example, replaced the old Iraqi currency, which bore the image of Saddam. They planned to restructure the Central Bank, which used to be under Saddam's control. U.S. officials also planned for a second round of reconstruction contracts, which they expected would help get Iraq's economy moving by funding many more construction and repair projects, which would, in turn, provide jobs for Iraqi workers. Interest in the projects among Iraqi and other businesses was high, and Sami al-Maajoun, the minister of labor and social affairs, says he is "very encouraged" by the American rebuilding efforts. "Iraqis are crying out for employment," he states. "We want to rebuild. Construction means jobs that will bring Iraq back to the situation it should have been in as far as its own wealth is concerned."[72]

Yet another goal of U.S. administrators in Iraq was to reduce Iraq's $120-billion debt. This, experts said, would give investors confidence that the country would be a stable place to put their money. President Bush hoped his envoy, former U.S. secretary of state James A. Baker III, would be able to successfully negotiate debt restructuring with the various countries involved. In late December 2003 and early January 2004, this hope was strengthened when France, Germany, Russia, and several Arab countries agreed to work with the United States on a substantial reduction of Iraq's debt.

A Free-Market Economy

America's long-term plan for rebuilding the Iraqi economy centered around efforts to privatize and restructure it. This involved shifting ownership of Iraq's industries from the state to private companies. It was hoped that one day Iraq would have a free-market economy similar to the U.S. economy. In a

Iraq's Boxing Team

The will to resume normal life was seen among Iraq's national boxing team, which decided to begin training for the 2004 Summer Olympic Games in Athens, Greece. Although they would have little time to train, the athletes were enthused by new equipment and salaries provided by the United States. This would be their first Olympic appearance since 1988. During Saddam Hussein's rule, his son Uday headed the Iraqi National Olympic Committee. Uday was known for not providing enough resources as well as for torturing and jailing athletes who failed to do well in competitions. In a December 2, 2003, article, the Associated Press quoted Iraqi boxing coach Abdul-Zahara Jawad as predicting, "With God's will and with the help of the Americans, we will achieve good results and raise the Iraqi flag in Athens."

free-market economy customers' demands for goods—rather than government quotas—determine what companies produce and how much they charge for their products and services. U.S. officials believed such a change was necessary to attract investment and make Iraq's industries competitive in the world economy.

Thus, government restrictions on trade, the flow of money, and foreign investment were nearly all ended. Foreign companies were encouraged to invest in and trade with Iraq: Taxes on foreign goods were cut to 5 percent, foreign banks were allowed to open branches and buy Iraqi banks, and foreigners were permitted to own 100 percent of Iraqi businesses. The United States hoped these changes would, over time, allow Iraqi companies to compete globally and lead to economic recovery.

However, the idea of allowing foreigners such a large economic stake in Iraq was troublesome to some Iraqi businesspeople. They claimed that opening Iraq to the global market would kill already-struggling Iraqi businesses by forcing them to compete with large foreign companies before they were ready to do so. Even Iraq's interim trade minister, Ali Abdul-Amir Allawi, warned that pushing the economy into a free-market system before it was ready could cause higher unemployment and heighten political instability. Arguing that Iraqi companies still face substantial obstacles, such as a lack of funding, technology, and management expertise, Allawi asserts, "The Iraqi private sector is extremely weak."[73]

Although opinions differ about timing and extent, everyone agrees that foreign investment is necessary to ensure a prosperous Iraq. Potential investors are already exploring opportunities. In late October 2003 about two hundred executives from oil, gas, financial, and other companies—representing forty-seven different countries—gathered for a meeting to discuss their interest in investing in Iraq. Surprisingly, Iraq's security problems at first did not present a major deterrent to some investors. According to Pedro Gonzalez-Haba, foreign affairs director of the Spanish Builders' Association, "Sure there's lack of security, but it's no worse than working in some Latin American countries or Africa."[74] Some potential investors even predicted that the Iraqi economy might transform quickly and, with the help of investment, privatization, and loans, perhaps even flourish as early as 2005. By the second investors' meeting in December 2003, however, the mood had shifted due to the worsening insurgency problem. As Naomi Klein, a reporter for the *Nation,* describes, "It seems finally to have dawned on the investment community that Iraq is not only an 'exciting emerging market'; it's also a country on the verge of civil war."[75]

Many observers say, therefore, that the keys to a robust Iraqi future continue to be political stability and restoration of security. Until a minimum level of security can be maintained, and a legitimate Iraqi government is elected, the country will continue to be viewed as unstable by the outside world. Whether America and its coalition partners can help achieve these goals remains to be seen.

★ Notes ★

Introduction: "A Long, Hard Slog"

1. Quoted in CNN.com, "Rumsfeld Predicts 'Long, Hard Slog' in Iraq," October 22, 2003. www.cnn.com.

Chapter 1: America's Fight with Iraq

2. Geoff Simons, *Iraq: From Sumer to Saddam.* New York: St. Martin's, 1994, p. 231.
3. Elaine Sciolino, *The Outlaw State.* New York: John Wiley & Sons, 1991, p. 88.
4. Efraim Karsh and Inari Rautsi, *Saddam: A Political Biography.* New York: Free Press, 1991, p. 178.
5. Con Coughlin, *Saddam: King of Terror.* New York: HarperCollins, 2002, p. 168.
6. Quoted in Dilip Hiro, *The Longest War: The Iran-Iraq Military Conflict.* New York: Routledge, Chapman & Hall, 1991, p. 35.
7. Kenneth R. Timmerman, *The Death Lobby: How the West Armed Iraq.* New York: Houghton Mifflin, 1991, p. x.
8. Quoted in Dilip Hiro, *Iraq: In the Eye of the Storm.* New York: Thunder's Mouth/ Nation Books, 2002, pp. 39–40.
9. The White House, "A Decade of Deception and Defiance," September 12, 2002. http://usinfo.state.gov.
10. George W. Bush, State of the Union address, Washington, D.C., January 29, 2002. http://usinfo.state.gov.
11. Bush, State of the Union address.

12. Dick Cheney, speech to the Veterans of Foreign Wars 103rd National Convention, Nashville, TN, August 26, 2002. www.guardian.co.uk.
13. George W. Bush, speech to the United Nations, New York, September 12, 2002. http://usinfo.state.gov.
14. Quoted in CNN.com, "Text of U.N. Resolution on Iraq," November 8, 2002. www.cnn.com.
15. Quoted in CNN.com, "U.S., U.K., Spain Draft Resolution on Iraq," February 24, 2003. www.cnn.com.
16. George W. Bush, speech to the nation broadcast on national television, January 3, 2003. http://usinfo.state.gov.
17. Quoted in CNN.com, "Bush Calls End to 'Major Combat,'" May 2, 2003. www.cnn.com.

Chapter 2: Chaos in Postwar Iraq

18. Associated Press, "Partial Count Finds Many Civilians Killed," *San Diego Union-Tribune,* June 11, 2003.
19. Reuters, "Red Cross Urges U.S. to Secure Baghdad's Hospitals," April 11, 2003.
20. Homayra Ziad, "Hunger, Fear, and Chaos Abound in Post-War Iraq, Says Returning Visitor," *Washington Report on Middle East Affairs,* July/August 2003.
21. Quoted in Edmund L. Andrews and Susan Sachs, "Iraq's Slide into Lawlessness

Squanders Good Will for U.S.," *New York Times,* May 17, 2003.

22. Quoted in Eric Schmitt, "Senators Sharply Criticize Iraq Rebuilding Efforts," *New York Times,* May 22, 2003.

23. Quoted in Michael Elliot, "So, What Went Wrong?" *Time,* October 6, 2003.

24. Quoted in Eric Schmitt and Joel Brinkley, "State Dept. Study Foresaw Trouble Now Plaguing Iraq," *New York Times,* October 19, 2003.

25. *New York Times,* "The Quest for Illicit Weapons," April 18, 2003.

26. Quoted in Lane DeGregory, "A Letter from Saddam Hussein?" *St. Petersburg (FL) Times,* May 6, 2003, p. 1D.

27. Quoted in Steve Gutkin, "Alleged Saddam Tape Calls for War," *Salt Lake Tribune,* July 5, 2003.

28. Quoted in Robert F. Worth, "7 GIs Injured in Iraq in 2 Separate Attacks; Possible Saddam Tape also Broadcast," *International Herald Tribune,* July 9, 2003, p. 3.

29. Quoted in Susan Sachs, "New Tape, Said to Be by Saddam, Assails U.S. and Iraqi Allies," *New York Times,* November 16, 2003.

Chapter 3: Growing Terrorism and Resistance

30. Quoted in Online News Hour Update, "Iraqi Interim Member Dies from Wounds," September 25, 2003. www.pbs.org.

31. Quoted in Dexter Filkins and Eric Schmitt, "Other Attacks Averted in Iraq, a General Says," *New York Times,* March 4, 2004.

32. George W. Bush, "President Holds Press Conference," Washington, D.C., October 28, 2003. www.whitehouse.gov.

33. George W. Bush, "President Bush Addresses United Nations General Assembly," New York, September 23, 2003. www.whitehouse.gov.

34. Quoted in CNN.com, "U.S. Links Zarqawi to Iraq Attacks," January 30, 2004. www.cnn.com.

35. Quoted in Douglas Jehl and Devid E. Sanger, "Iraqis' Bitterness Is Called Bigger Threat than Terror," *New York Times,* September 17, 2003.

36. Quoted in Dexter Filkins, "Attacks on G.I.'s in Mosul Rise as Good Will Fades," *New York Times,* November 27, 2003.

37. Quoted in Wesley Pruden, "'A Hopeful Day Has Arrived' in Iraq," *Washington Times,* December 15, 2003.

38. Quoted in *Boston Herald,* "Saddam Captured, a New Iraq Begins," December 15, 2003, p. 42.

Chapter 4: Iraq: An American Responsibility

39. George W. Bush, "President's Statement on U.N. Vote Lifting Sanctions on Iraq," May 22, 2003. www.whitehouse.gov.

40. Quoted in Felicity Barringer, "U.N. Vote on Iraq Ends Sanctions and Grants U.S. Wide Authority," *New York Times,* May 22, 2003.

41. Quoted in Reuters, "Full Text from Security Council Resolution Ending U.N. Sanctions on Iraq," *New York Times,* May 23, 2003.

42. Bush, "President Bush Addresses United Nations General Assembly."

43. Quoted in Bob Herbert, "Hard Sell on Iraq," *New York Times,* October 10, 2003.

44. Herbert, "Hard Sell on Iraq."

45. Quoted in Herbert Docena, "Spoilers Gatecrash the Iraq Spoilers Party," *Asia Times Online,* October 28, 2003. www.a times.com.

46. Thomas L. Friedman, "You Gotta Have Friends," *New York Times,* November 20, 2003.

47. George W. Bush, "President Addresses the Nation," Washington, D.C., September 7, 2003. www.whitehouse.gov.

48. Quoted in Richard S. Dunham, Howard Gleckman, and Stan Crock, "The High Cost of War," *Business Week,* September 22, 2003.

49. Bush, "President Addresses the Nation."

Chapter 5: Creating a New Iraqi Government

50. Quoted in Bruce Fein, "A Judicious Change of Course," *Washington Times,* May 20, 2003.

51. Quoted in Edmund L. Andrews, "Shiite Group Says U.S. Is Reneging on Interim Rule," *New York Times,* May 18, 2003.

52. Quoted in Patrick E. Tyler, "Iraq Leaders Seek Greater Role Now in Running Nation," *New York Times,* September 27, 2003.

53. Quoted in Bob Wing, "Bush Foreign Policy Stalls as Costs Soar," *War Times,* October/November 2003. www.war-times.org.

54. Quoted in Susan Sachs and Joel Brinkley, "Iraqi Leaders Seek Power Before Drafting a Charter," *New York Times,* November 13, 2003.

55. Quoted in Eric Marquardt, "Al-Sistani's Call for Democratic Elections," *Progress Report.* www.progress.org.

56. Quoted in Fiona O'Brien, "Iraqis Demand Elections, Oppose U.S. Political Plan," Reuters, January 19, 2004. www.boston.com.

57. Quoted in Alex Berenson, "Iraq's Shiites Insist on Democracy. Washington Cringes," *New York Times,* November 30, 2003.

58. Quoted in Berenson, "Iraq's Shiites Insist on Democracy."

59. Quoted in Patrick E. Tyler, "Iraqi Groups Badly Divided over How to Draft a Charter," *New York Times,* September 30, 2003.

60. Quoted in *Charleston Post and Courier,* "Officials Fear Popular Elections Could Create Theocracy," December 7, 2003. www.charleston.net.

61. Quoted in Thomas L. Friedman, "God and Man in Baghdad," *New York Times,* December 4, 2003.

62. Friedman, "God and Man in Baghdad."

63. Quoted in Christine Spolar, "Iraqis Shelve Disputes, Sign Charter," *Chicago Tribune,* March 9, 2004.

64. Quoted in Rajiv Chandrasekaran, "Iraqi Council Signs Charter," *Washington Post,* March 9, 2004.

Chapter 6: Reconstruction Efforts

65. Quoted in James Glanz, "Rebuilding Iraq Takes Courage, Cash, and Improvisation," *New York Times,* November 30, 2003.

66. Quoted in Glanz, "Rebuilding Iraq Takes Courage, Cash, and Improvisation."

67. Art Messer, "The Straight Scoop: A Seabee's Firsthand Account of Life in Iraq," Defend America: U.S. Department of Defense News About the War on Terrorism, www.defendamerica.mil/articles/aug2003./a080703c.html.

68. Quoted in John Tierney, "Editing Saddam Out of School Books," *South End Online,* October 2, 2003. www.southend.wayne.edu.

69. Quoted in Joel Brinkley, "Iraqis Get Used to Life Without Hussein, and Many Find They Like It," *New York Times,* October 26, 2003.

70. *Economist,* "Amid the Bombs and the Rubble, the Country Is Still Slowly on the Mend," November 1, 2003.

71. Quoted in Edward Wong, "Salaries Rise, but So Does Desire for Security," *International Herald Tribune,* December 9, 2003. www.iht.com.

72. Quoted in Michael Janofsky, "At U.S. Meeting, Iraq Appears Open for Business," *New York Times,* December 5, 2003.

73. Quoted in Thomas Crampton, "Iraqi Urges Caution on Free Markets," *International Herald Tribune,* October 13, 2003. www.iht.com.

74. Quoted in Dale Fuchs, "Companies Everywhere Seek Role in Iraq," *New York Times,* October 25, 2003.

75. Naomi Klein, "Risky Business. Rebuilding Iraq 2 Meeting for Potential Iraq Contractors," *Nation,* January 5, 2004.

★ Chronology ★

1920

Iraq is created in its current boundaries as a British colonial monarchy.

1958

Iraq becomes a republic. The monarchy is overthrown in a military coup led by General Abdul Karim Kassem.

1968

The Baath Party seizes power in Iraq, Saddam Hussein's cousin Ahmad Hasan al-Bakr becomes president. Saddam rises as a key leader in the party.

1979

Saddam becomes president and purges all opposition through terror. The Iran-Iraq War begins.

1984

UN investigators report that Iraq is using mustard gas and nerve gas in the Iran-Iraq War.

1988

Saddam uses chemical weapons against civilian Kurds in the town of Halabja, leaving five thousand dead and ten thousand wounded.

1990

August 2: Iraq invades Kuwait

August 6: The UN Security Council passes Resolution 661, imposing economic sanctions.

November 29: The Security Council passes Resolution 678, authorizing member states to use force unless Iraq leaves Kuwait by January 15, 1991.

1991

April 4: The UN Special Committee on Iraq (UNSCOM) is created to monitor Iraq's weapons of mass destruction programs.

1999–2000

The United States and Britain pursue an aggressive bombing campaign against Iraq.

2001

The United States is attacked by terrorists on September 11.

2002

January 29: President George W. Bush announces in his State of the Union speech that Iraq is one of three countries forming an "axis of evil."

September 12: President Bush addresses the United Nations, outlining Saddam's disregard for multiple UN resolutions and asking for UN help with the Iraqi threat of weapons of mass destruction.

November 8: The United Nations passes Resolution 1441, giving Saddam one last chance to disarm. The UN Monitoring, Verification, and Inspection Commission (UNMOVIC) begins inspections in late November.

2003

January: UNMOVIC and the International Atomic Energy Agency report to the United Nations that they have received access to Iraqi facilities but that no weapons of mass destruction have been discovered.

February 24: The United States, Britain, and Spain circulate a second UN resolution to authorize war against Iraq, but it does not pass.

March 19: The war begins.

March 23: Allied troops encounter unexpected resistance from Iraqi fighters.

April 9: Iraqi citizens and U.S. Marines topple a statue of Saddam in Baghdad.

April 15: The U.S. Pentagon says the main fighting in Iraq is finished, and President Bush declares that "the regime of Saddam Hussein is no more."

April 30: A newspaper prints a handwritten letter said to be written and signed by Saddam that urges Iraqis to rebel against the invaders.

May 16: Administrator L. Paul Bremer announces the coalition will remain in charge of Iraq for an indefinite period.

May 22: The UN Security Council votes unanimously to allow the United States and Britain to occupy and rebuild Iraq and to end economic sanctions.

May–June: Reconstruction begins to restore order, repair electrical and other utilities, and get Iraqi oil flowing.

June 22: Iraq exports its first oil since the end of the war.

June 30: Iraq's leading moderate Shia cleric, Grand Ayatollah Ali al-Sistani, asserts that Iraqis should elect the drafters of their constitution.

July 5: Guerrillas bomb a graduation ceremony for the first class of American-trained police officers in Iraq.

August 7: A car bomb is detonated outside of the Jordanian embassy in Baghdad.

August 15–17: A water pipeline in Baghdad and an oil pipeline in northern Iraq, important for carrying Iraqi oil into Turkey, are blown up.

August 19: A suicide bomber attacks the UN headquarters in Baghdad.

September 1: The Iraqi Governing Council (IGC) names a twenty-five-member cabinet to take over the day-to-day running of the government.

September 21: Akila al-Hashemi, a member of the IGC, is shot and killed.

September 23: President Bush, in a speech to the UN General Assembly, urges the United Nations to help Iraq and emphasizes that a democratic Iraq would transform the Middle East.

October 9: Gunmen shoot a Spanish intelligence officer, José Antonio Bernal Gomez, and an insurgent sets off a car bomb in a crowd of Iraqi policemen.

October 14: A bomb explodes close to the Turkish embassy in Baghdad.

October 17: The U.S. Congress approves President Bush's request for $87 billion in emergency spending for military operations and reconstruction in Iraq and Afghanistan for the year 2004.

October 27: Suicide car bombers attack the offices of the International Committee of the Red Cross and four Iraqi police stations.

November 2: Insurgents shoot down an American helicopter near Fallujah.

November 12: The United States announces it will speed up Iraqi elections and turn civilian authority over to a temporary Iraqi government by July 2004. U.S. forces begin more aggressive campaigns against insurgents.

November 30: Iraqi guerrillas shoot grenades at two cars carrying eight Spanish intelligence officers in Mahmudiya, kill two Japanese diplomats in an ambush in Tikrit, and shoot two South Korean civilians who were assisting Iraq with electrical repairs.

December 5: President Bush appoints former U.S. secretary of state James A. Baker III to negotiate a restructuring of Iraq's debts.

December 9: The U.S. Pentagon announces a new policy of limiting future U.S. reconstruction contracts to the countries that have given political or military aid to Iraq.

December 13: U.S. forces capture Saddam.

2004

January 19: UN secretary-general Kofi Annan agrees to send UN elections experts to Iraq.

January 23: David Kay, head of the U.S. team searching for weapons of mass destruction in Iraq, resigns and concludes that Iraq had no such weapons when war was declared in 2003.

February 8: U.S. troops find a letter, purportedly written by Islamic extremist Abu Musab al-Zarqawi to senior leaders of al Qaeda. It urged attacks on Iraqi Shias in order to start a civil war in Iraq.

February 23: The United Nations reports that elections are impossible by June 30 and offers to help Iraqis find a way to establish an interim government. They say elections can be conducted later.

March 2: Bombs explode during Shia Muslim religious ceremonies in Baghdad and Karbala, killing at least 143 Iraqis.

March 8: The Iraqi Governing Council signs an interim constitution that will serve as the framework for the government through 2005. Shia members sign the document, even though they have reservations.

☆ For Further Reading ☆

Books

Fred Bratman, *War in the Persian Gulf.* Brookfield, CT: Millbrook, 1991. This is a young-adult selection that discusses the 1990–1991 Persian Gulf War, from the Iraqi invasion of Kuwait in 1990 to the allied victory in 1991.

Joseph Braude, *The New Iraq: Rebuilding the Country for Its People, the Middle East, and the World.* New York: Basic Books, 2003. This book describes the effects of wars, sanctions, and Saddam Hussein's rule on Iraq's economy and the challenges that lie ahead for the postwar reconstruction of the country.

Richard Butler, *The Greatest Threat: Iraq, Weapons of Mass Destruction, and the Crisis of Global Security.* New York: Public Affairs, 2000. This book is written by the head of the UN weapons inspection team that searched Iraq for weapons of mass destruction during the 1990s. It discusses that effort and the team's findings.

Paul J. Deegan, *Saddam Hussein.* Edina, MN: Abdo & Daughters, 1990. This is a young-adult book that examines the life of Saddam.

Susan M. Hassig and Laith Muhmood al-Adely, *Iraq.* New York: Benchmark Books, 2004. A book for young readers that explores the geography, history, government, economy, people, and culture of Iraq.

Stacy Taus-Bolstad, *Iraq in Pictures.* Minneapolis: Lerner, 2004. A pictorial exploration of Iraq's land, history, government, culture, and economy.

Web Sites

Coalition Provisional Authority (www.cpa-iraq.org). A Web site set up by the U.S. occupation authority in Iraq.

The Iraq Foundation (www.iraqfoundation.org). A nonprofit, nongovernmental organization working for democracy and human rights in Iraq.

Iraq Today (www.iraq-today.com). The Web site for Iraq's first national English-language newspaper of the post-Saddam era, founded and staffed by Iraqis.

The Nonviolence Web, Iraq Crisis Anti war Homepage (www.nonviolence.org). Home to dozens of major U.S. peace groups, with articles and information about postwar Iraq.

U.S. Central Intelligence Agency (CIA) (www.cia.gov). A government Web site providing geographical, political, economic, and other information on the country of Iraq.

U.S. Department of State, International Information Programs (http://usinfo.state.gov). A government Web site providing information about current political and human rights issues involving Iraq.

☆ Works Consulted ☆

Books

Said K. Aburish, *Saddam Hussein: The Politics of Revenge*. New York: Bloomsbury, 2000. This is a biography of Saddam covering his rise to power and his tenure as president of Iraq.

Con Coughlin, *Saddam: King of Terror*. New York: HarperCollins, 2002. A biography of Saddam, who ruled Iraq for decades until the United States overthrew his regime in 2003.

Dilip Hiro, *Iraq: In the Eye of the Storm*. New York: Thunder's Mouth/Nation Books, 2002. An examination of the events leading up to and following the Persian Gulf War of 1991.

———, *The Longest War: The Iran-Iraq Military Conflict*. New York: Routledge, Chapman & Hall, 1991. A detailed discussion of the Iran-Iraq War, its causes, and its ramifications.

Efraim Karsh and Inari Rautsi, *Saddam Hussein: A Political Biography*. New York: Free Press, 1991. A biography of Saddam tracing his activities up to and including the 1991 Persian Gulf War.

Helen Chapin Metz, ed., *Iraq: A Country Study*. Washington, DC: U.S. Library of Congress, 1988. This is a Library of Congress study and report on Iraq, providing a good overview of its history, society, economy, government, military, and foreign policy.

Elaine Sciolino, *The Outlaw State*. New York: John Wiley & Sons, 1991. An account of Saddam and his determination to turn Iraq into a superpower in the Middle East.

Geoff Simons, *Iraq: From Sumer to Saddam*. New York: St. Martin's, 1994. Written by a freelance author and former editor, this book provides a broad history of Iraq, from ancient times to the present, with a particular focus on twentieth-century events.

Kenneth R. Timmerman, *The Death Lobby: How the West Armed Iraq*. New York: Houghton Mifflin, 1991. A detailed description of Iraq's arms buildup and the role the United States and other western powers played in supplying weapons to Saddam.

Periodicals

Daniel Benjamin and Steven Simon, "The Real Worry: In Iraq We Have Created a New 'Field of Jihad,'" *Time*, September 1, 2003.

Michael Duffy, "Weapons of Mass Disappearance," *Time*, June 9, 2003.

Richard S. Dunham, Howard Gleckman, and Stan Crock, "The High Cost of War," *Business Week*, September 22, 2003.

Earth Island Journal, "The Cost of War," Summer 2003.

Economist, "Amid the Bombs and the Rubble, the Country Is Still Slowly on the Mend," November 1, 2003.

———, "The Other Battle: Humanitarian Assistance," April 5, 2003.

Michael Elliot, "So, What Went Wrong?" *Time,* October 6, 2003.

Adnan R. Khan, "Killing Was Just a Game: Hundreds of Iraqis Are Digging Through Mass Graves in Search of Relatives, *Maclean's,* June 2, 2003.

Naomi Klein, "Risky Business. Rebuilding Iraq 2 Meeting for Potential Iraq Contractors," *Nation,* January 5, 2004.

Gabriel Kolko, "Iraq, the United States, and the End of the European Coalition," *Journal of Contemporary Asia,* August 2003.

Maryam Moody and Karla Mantilla, "After the War: Women in Iraq (Interview)," *Off Our Backs,* July/August 2003.

Rod Nordland and Michael Hirsh, "The $87 Billion Money Pit," *Newsweek,* November 3, 2003.

Bruce Nussbaum, "Iraq: Hard Lessons and How to Use Them," *Business Week,* September 22, 2003.

Simon Robinson, "Progress, Inch by Inch," *Time,* October 6, 2003.

Kevin Whitelaw and Mark Mazzetti, "Law and Disorder," *U.S. News & World Report,* May 26, 2003.

Homayra Ziad, "Hunger, Fear, and Chaos Abound in Post-War Iraq, Says Returning Visitor," *Washington Report on Middle East Affairs,* July/August 2003.

Stephen Zunes, "Foreign Policy by Catharsis: The Failure of U.S. Policy Toward Iraq," *Arab Studies Quarterly,* Fall 2001.

Newspapers

Edmund L. Andrews, "Shiite Group Says U.S. Is Reneging on Interim Rule," *New York Times,* May 18, 2003.

Edmund L. Andrews and Susan Sachs, "Iraq's Slide into Lawlessness Squanders Good Will for U.S.," *New York Times,* May 17, 2003.

Erin E. Arvedlund, "For Oil Contracts, Russia Will Waive Most of Iraq's $8 Billion Debt," *New York Times,* December 23, 2003.

Associated Press, "Bush Expresses Less Certainty on Iraq Arms," *New York Times,* January 27, 2004.

———, "Bush Sees Attackers as Growing Desperate Amid Progress in Iraq," *New York Times,* October 27, 2003.

———, "Cleric Joins Opposition to Iraq Plan," *New York Times,* December 3, 2003.

———, "Ex-Minister: Saddam May Have Billions," *New York Times,* December 4, 2003.

———, "Israeli Raid in Syria Alarms Arab World," *New York Times,* October 6, 2003.

———, "Looted Relics Returned to Iraqi Museum," *New York Times,* November 11, 2003.

———, "Lost Iraqi Treasures Found," *New York Times,* June 7, 2003.

———, "Partial Count Finds Many Civilians Killed," *San Diego Union-Tribune,* June 11, 2003.

———, "Public Tribunal That Would Withstand Scrutiny Is Goal," *New York Times,* December 15, 2003.

———, "Scientists to Excavate Iraqi Graves," *New York Times,* December 6, 2003.

————, "Sen. Clinton Raps Bush's Iraq Strategy," *New York Times,* December 1, 2003.

————, "Survey: Saddam Killed 61,000 in Baghdad," *New York Times,* December 9, 2003.

————, "U.S.: Fewer Attacks Since Saddam Capture," *New York Times,* January 13, 2004.

Felicity Barringer, "U.N. Vote on Iraq Ends Sanctions and Grants U.S. Wide Authority," *New York Times,* May 22, 2003.

Milt Bearden, "Iraqi Insurgents Take a Page from the Afghan 'Freedom Fighter,'" *New York Times,* November 9, 2003.

Alex Berenson, "Iraq's Shiites Insist on Democracy. Washington Cringes," *New York Times,* November 30, 2003.

Raymond Bonner, "Guerrillas in Iraq Tap Unsecured Arms Caches, Officials Say," *New York Times,* October 14, 2003.

————, "U.S. Can't Locate Missiles Once Held in Iraq Arsenal," *New York Times,* October 8, 2003.

Boston Herald, "Saddam Captured, a New Iraq Begins," December 15, 2003.

Joel Brinkley, "Few Signs of Infiltration by Foreign Fighters in Iraq," *New York Times,* November 19, 2003.

————, "Iraqi Governing Council Voices Support for June Elections," *New York Times,* November 30, 2003.

————, "Iraqis Get Used to Life Without Hussein, and Many Find They Like It," *New York Times,* October 26, 2003.

Joel Brinkley and Ian Fisher, "U.S. Plan in Iraq to Shift Control Hits Major Snag," *New York Times,* November 27, 2003.

Rajiv Chandrasekaran, "Iraqi Council Signs Charter," *Washington Post,* March 9, 2004.

Lynette Clemetson, "Thousands in D.C. Protest Iraq War Plans," *New York Times,* January 20, 2003.

Lane DeGregory, "A Letter from Saddam Hussein?" *St. Petersburg (FL) Times,* May 6, 2003.

Bruce Fein, "A Judicious Change of Course," *Washington Times,* May 20, 2003.

Dexter Filkins, "Attacks on G.I.'s in Mosul Rise as Good Will Fades," *New York Times,* November 27, 2003.

Dexter Filkins and Eric Schmitt, "Other Attacks Averted in Iraq, a General Says," *New York Times,* March 4, 2004.

Ian Fisher, "Attacks Go On; Car Bomb Kills 6 Iraqi Officers," *New York Times,* December 16, 2003.

Ian Fisher and Christine Hauser, "2 Car Bombers Attack Iraqi Police, as Insurgency Continues," *New York Times,* December 15, 2003.

Thomas L. Friedman, "God and Man in Baghdad," *New York Times,* December 4, 2003.

————, "Moment of Truth," *New York Times,* December 18, 2003.

————, "You Gotta Have Friends," *New York Times,* November 20, 2003.

Dale Fuchs, "Companies Everywhere Seek Role in Iraq," *New York Times,* October 25, 2003.

James Glanz, "Rebuilding Iraq Takes Courage, Cash, and Improvisation," *New York Times,* November 30, 2003.

Michael R. Gordon, "For U.S. Foes, a Major Blow: Fighters Now Lack a Symbol," *New York Times,* December 15, 2003.

Steve Gutkin, "Alleged Saddam Tape Calls for War," *Salt Lake Tribune,* July 5, 2003.

Bob Herbert, "Hard Sell on Iraq," *New York Times,* October 10, 2003.

Michael Janofsky, "At U.S. Meeting, Iraq Appears Open for Business," *New York Times,* December 5, 2003.

Douglas Jehl, "More Proof of Iraq-Qaeda Link, or Not?" *New York Times,* November 20, 2003.

———, "U.S. Sees Evidence of Overcharging in Iraq Contract," *New York Times,* December 12, 2003.

Douglas Jehl and Devid E. Sanger, "Iraqis' Bitterness Is Called Bigger Threat than Terror," *New York Times,* September 17, 2003.

Neil A. Lewis, "Iraqis Just Recently Set Rules to Govern Tribunal," *New York Times,* December 15, 2003.

Neil MacFarouhar, "Deadly Bombing of Saudi Homes Sours al Qaeda Sympathizers," *New York Times,* November 10, 2003.

Christopher Marquis, "Powell Admits No Hard Proof in Linking Iraq to al Qaeda," *New York Times,* January 9, 2004.

———, "Russia Sees Iraqi Debt Relief as Link to Oil, U.S. Aides Say," *New York Times,* January 17, 2004.

New York Times, "Cleric Backs U.S. Voting Plan," December 3, 2003.

———, "In Bush's Words: 'Iraqi Democracy Will Succeed,'" November 6, 2003.

———, "In Bush's Words: 'We Have the Right Strategy' on Iraq," October 28, 2003.

———, "The Quest for Illicit Weapons," April 18, 2003.

Norimitsu Onishi, "Japan Says It Will Forgive Most of Debt Owed by Iraq," *New York Times,* December 30, 2003.

Wesley Pruden, "'A Hopeful Day Has Arrived' in Iraq," *Washington Times,* December 15, 2003.

Reuters, "Full Text from Security Council Resolution Ending U.N. Sanctions on Iraq," *New York Times,* May 23, 2003.

———, "Red Cross Urges U.S. to Secure Baghdad's Hospitals," April 11, 2003.

James Risen and Judith Miller, "No Illicit Arms Found in Iraq, U.S. Inspector Tells Congress," *New York Times,* October 2, 2003.

Susan Sachs, "New Tape, Said to Be by Hussein, Assails U.S. and Iraqi Allies," *New York Times,* November 16, 2003.

Susan Sachs and Joel Brinkley, "Iraqi Leaders Seek Power Before Drafting a Charter," *New York Times,* November 13, 2003.

William Safire, "Clear Ties of Terror," *New York Times,* January 27, 2003.

David E. Sanger, "Bush's Day at the U.N.: It's Chilly, Still, There," *New York Times,* October 24, 2003.

Eric Schmitt, "Cheney Asserts No Responsible Leader Could Have Ignored Danger from Iraq," *New York Times,* July 24, 2003.

———, "Senators Sharply Criticize Iraq Rebuilding Efforts," *New York Times,* May 22, 2003.

Eric Schmitt and Joel Brinkley, "State Dept. Study Foresaw Trouble Now Plaguing Iraq," *New York Times,* October 19, 2003.

Marlise Simons, "In the Street, Across Europe, a Weekend of Antiwar Rallies," *New York Times,* January 20, 2003.

Christine Spolar, "Iraqis Shelve Disputes, Sign Charter," *Chicago Tribune,* March 9, 2004.

Richard W. Stevenson, "Remember 'Weapons of Mass Destruction'? For Bush, They Are a Nonissue," *New York Times,* December 18, 2003.

Patrick E. Tyler, "Iraqi Groups Badly Divided over How to Draft a Charter," *New York Times,* September 30, 2003.

———, "Iraq Leaders Seek Greater Role Now in Running Nation," *New York Times,* September 27, 2003.

Don Van Natta Jr., "High Payments to Halliburton for Fuel in Iraq," *New York Times,* December 10, 2003.

Steven R. Weisman, "Arab Nations Agree to Reduce Debt Owed by Iraq," *New York Times,* January 22, 2004.

———, "Betting on Democracy in the Muslim World," *New York Times,* November 9, 2003.

Robert F. Worth, "7 GIs Injured in Iraq in 2 Separate Attacks; Possible Saddam Tape also Broadcast," *International Herald Tribune,* July 9, 2003.

Internet Sources

Arab Gateway, "Iraq: Governing Council, July 2003," September 3, 2003. www.albab.com.

BBC, "Text of 'Saddam Hussein Letter,'" April 30, 2003. http://news.bbc.co.uk.

George W. Bush, address to a joint session of Congress and the nation, Washington, D.C., September 20, 2001. http://usinfo.state.gov.

———, "President Addresses the Nation," Washington, D.C., September 7, 2003. www.whitehouse.gov.

———, "President Bush Addresses United Nations General Assembly," New York, September 23, 2003. www.whitehouse.gov

———, "President Holds Press Conference," Washington, D.C., October 28, 2003. www.whitehouse.gov.

———, "President's Statement on U.N. Vote Lifting Sanctions on Iraq," May 22, 2003. www.whitehouse.gov.

———, speech to the nation broadcast on national television, January 3, 2003. http://usinfo.state.gov.

———, speech to the United Nations, New York, September 12, 2002. http://usinfo.state.gov.

———, State of the Union address, Washington, D.C., January 29, 2002. http://usinfo.state.gov.

Charleston Post and Courier, "Officials Fear Popular Elections Could Create Theocracy," December 7, 2003. www.charleston.net.

Dick Cheney, speech to the Veterans of Foreign Wars 103rd National Convention, Nashville, TN, August 26, 2002. www.guardian.co.uk.

CNN.com, "Bush Calls End to 'Major Combat,'" May 2, 2003. www.cnn.com.

———, "Rumsfeld Predicts 'Long, Hard Slog' in Iraq," October 22, 2003. www.cnn.com.

———, "European Protesters Fill Cities," February 15, 2003. www.cnn.com.

———, "Text of U.N. Resolution on Iraq," November 8, 2002. www.cnn.com

———, "U.S. Links Zarqawi to Iraq Attacks," January 30, 2004. www.cnn.com.

———, "U.S., U.K., Spain, Draft Resolution on Iraq," February 24, 2003. www.cnn.com.

Thomas Crampton, "Iraqi Urges Caution on Free Markets," *International Herald Tribune,* October 13, 2003. www.iht.com.

John F. Cullinan, "Putting It in Ink: Getting Iraq's Constitution Right," *National Review Online,* October 6, 2003. www.nationalreview.com.

Herbert Docena, "Spoilers Gatecrash the Iraq Spoilers Party," *Asia Times Online,* October 28, 2003. www.atimes.com.

Phillip Kurata, "Iraq National Symphony Performs in Washington," U.S. Department of State, December 9, 2003. http://usinfo.state.gov.

Eric Marquardt, "Al-Sistani's Call for Democratic Elections," *Progress Report.* www.progress.org.

Ali A. Mazmi, "Islamic and Western Values," Al-Hewar Center, September/October 1997. www.alhewar.com.

Art Messer, "The Straight Scoop: A Seabee's Firsthand Account of Life in Iraq," Defend America: U.S. Department of Defense News About the War on Terrorism, www.defendamerica.mil/articles/aug2003./9080703c.htm

Middle East Reference, "Iraq's Governing Council," August 3, 2003. http://middleeastreference.org.uk.

Fiona O'Brien, "Iraqis Demand Elections, Oppose U.S. Political Plan," Reuters, January 19, 2004. www.boston.com.

Online News Hour Update, "Iraqi Interim Member Dies from Wounds," September 25, 2003. www.pbs.org.

Sharon Otterman, "Iraq: Grand Ayatollah Ali al-Sistani," Council on Foreign Relations, www.cfr.org.

John Tierney, "Editing Saddam Out of School Books," *South End Online,* October 2, 2003. www.southend.wayne.edu.

UN Association of the United States of America, "U.N. Secretary-General Kofi Annan: Remarks at the General Assembly of the United Nations," September 23, 2003. www.unausa.org.

UN Security Council, "Resolutions 2003," www.un.org.

USAID, "Transcript: Infrastructure Restoration Update," July 1, 2003. http://gopher.info.usaid.gov.

The White House, "A Decade of Deception and Defiance," September 12, 2002. http://usinfo.state.gov.

Bob Wing, "Bush Foreign Policy Stalls as Costs Soar," *War Times,* October/November 2003. www.war-times.org.

Edward Wong, "Salaries Rise, but So Does Desire for Security," *International Herald Tribune,* December 9, 2003. www.iht.com.

★ Index ★

Aabadi, Hayder Awad, 68
allies, 18
Annan, Kofi, 57, 61, 72
anthrax, 22
anti–Iraq War protests, 25
Arab Fund for Social and Economic
  Development, 54
"axis of evil," 21, 62
Aziz, Tariq, 37

Baath Party, 15–16
Bajaji, Adnan, 66
Baker, James A., III, 89
Bakr, Ahmad Hasan al-, 15
banking, 89
Barzani, Massoud, 76
Bechtel, 80
Berwari, Nesreen M. Siddeek, 77
Biden, Joseph R., Jr., 33
bin Laden, Osama, 46–47
biological weapons, 22, 34–36
Blair, Tony, 23
Bremer, L. Paul, III, 33, 41, 66–67, 87
Bush, George W.
  announcement of Iraq War plans by,
    24, 26
  on "axis of evil," 21–22
  on benefits of a stabilized Iraq, 55
  business contracts for Iraq occupation
    projects and, 61
  on capture of Saddam Hussein, 52
  coalition for Iraq War and, 24
  on cost of Iraq War, 58
  on danger of weapons of mass
    destruction, 22
  on end of combat operations in Iraq,
    27
  on Iraqi resistance fighters, 45
  on Saddam Hussein violations of UN
    resolutions, 20, 24
  on UN resolution granting U.S. full
    authority in Iraq, 53
  weapons of mass destruction and,
    11–12
business activity, 86–90

casualties, 48
Central Bank of Iraq, 89
Central Intelligence Agency (CIA), 35
Chalabi, Ahmad, 66
challenges. See problems
chemical weapons, 34–36, 37
Cheney, Dick, 22–23, 61
Christians, 67
"coalition of the willing," 24
Coalition Provisional Authority (CPA),
  67
communications systems, 81–82
constitution, 67, 69, 75–76
cost, of rebuilding Iraq, 56–61, 82

Coughlin, Con, 17
criticism, of U.S.-Iraq policies
  failure to locate weapons of mass
    destruction, 34–36
  by France, 53–54
  by IGC, 68–69
  by U.S. taxpayers, 59–61
currency, 89

deficit, 60
dictatorship, 15–17

economics, 86–90
  see also cost, of rebuilding Iraq
education, 85
elections, 67
electricity, 77–79, 80–81
ethnic groups, 69
  see also Kurds; Shias; Sunnis
everyday life, 85–86
exit strategies, 11, 13, 70

Feldman, Noah, 74
financial aid, 56–58
  see also cost, of rebuilding Iraq
food-ration programs, 85
free-market economy, 89–90
Friedman, Thomas L., 58, 75

Garner, Jay, 33, 64
Ghul, Hassan, 47
González-Haba, Pedro, 90
government
  election difficulties and, 70–72
  Islam and, 73–75
  role of religion in, 69

transitional government
  announcement, 70
  women and, 86
  see also constitution; dictatorship;
    elections; Iraqi Governing Council
guerrilla fighters, 27
  see also resistance, to U.S. occupation

Hadi, Ahmad, 72
Hakim, Abdul Aziz al-, 74
Hakim, Mohammad Baqir al-, 41
Halliburton, 61
Hashemi, Akila al-, 41
Herbert, Bob, 56
holy war (jihad), 47–48
Hussein, Qusay, 37
Hussein, Saddam
  Bush, and, 11
  capture of, 49, 52
  communications from, 37–38
  defiance of, 21
  education in Iraq and, 85
  humanitarian aid efforts and, 21
  Kurds and, 64
  Kuwait and, 18
  policies of, 15–17
  sons of, 37
  survival of Iraq War by, 36–38
  UN weapons inspectors and, 20
Hussein, Uday, 37, 89

Independent Democrats Movement,
  66
infrastructure, 77–82
insurgents, 44
  see also resistance, to U.S. occupation

International Atomic Energy Agency
  (IAEA), 24
International Committee of the Red
  Cross, 44
International Money Fund (IMF), 54, 57
Iran-Iraq War, 17–18
Iraq
  anti-American feelings in, 50–51
  ethnic groups of, 63–64, 69
  hardships of people of, 20–21
  nations contributing to aid for, 30
  Olympic Games and, 89
  political instability of, 13–14
  rebuilding authority in, 53
  sanctions against, 20–21
  terrorism link and, 23
  weapons inspections and, 24
Iraqi Governing Council (IGC)
  assassination attempts and, 67–68
  attacks on, 41
  cabinet ministry naming and, 67
  composition of, 66, 67
  criticism of American control by, 68–69
  demonstrations against, 66
  economic rebuilding and, 87
  election planning and, 67
  formation of, 65–67
  limitations on, 65, 66
  Saddam Hussein and, 38
Iraqi National Congress, 66
Iraqi National Olympic Committee, 89
Iraqi resistance. See resistance, to U.S.
  occupation
Iraqi Symphony, 83
Iraq Stabilization Group, 34
Iraq War

beginning of, 26
casualties in, 28
combat strategies of, 26–27
criticism of, 12, 23–24
impact of, on Iraqi people, 28–30
summary of, 11
U.S. victory in, 27
Islam, 69, 73–75
  see also Muslims; religion; Shias; Sunnis

Al Jazeera (television station), 37–38
jihad (holy war), 47–48

Karsh, Efraim, 16–17
Kay, David, 35
Khomeini, Ayatollah, 17–18
Klein, Naomi, 90
Kurata, Phillip, 83
Kurds
  concerns about future of, 13
  constitution and, 75–76
  demands of, regarding new Iraq
    government, 72
  history of, 64
  IGC and, 66
  recovery of, from war, 86
  Saddam Hussein regime and, 21, 37
Kuwait, 18, 19

Lugar, Richard G., 32–33

Maajoun, Sami al-, 89
Madrid conference, 56–57
Mahdi, Adel Abdel, 66, 69
Majid, Ali Hassan al- ("Chemical Ali"),
  37

"Martyrs of Saddam," 27
Mello, Sergio Vieira de, 54
military, Iraqi, 87–88
military assistance, 55–56
money, 56–58
  see also cost, of rebuilding Iraq;
    currency
Muslims, 63–64, 69
see also Islam; religion; Shias; Sunnis

Nakash, Yitzhak, 75
Nation (magazine), 90
nerve gas, 22
New York Times (newspaper), 15, 34, 56,
  58, 75
nuclear weapons, 22, 34–36
  see also weapons of mass destruction

Odierno, Raymond T., 52
oil, 54, 82, 84–85
oil-for-food program (OFFP), 21, 29, 30
Operation Desert Fox, 21
Operation Desert Storm, 18
Operation Iraqi Freedom, 26–27
Operation Iron Hammer, 48–52
opposition. See criticism, of U.S.-Iraq
  policies; resistance, to U.S. occupation

Pachachi, Adnan, 42, 75
Patriotic Union of Kurdistan, 66
Persian Gulf War, 18–21
Pleuger, Gunter, 54
police, 87–88
Powell, Colin, 57, 83
problems
  debt, 89

ethnic and religious diversity, 69
general discussion of, 11–13, 28–34
infrastructure damage, 77–78
looting, 33–34, 78–79
rebellions by Iraqi Governing Council
  (IGC), 68–69
religious disagreements, 72–73
sabotage, 79–80
security, 33–34, 79–80
State Department predictions of,
  33–34
unemployment, 86–88, 89
  see also resistance, to U.S. occupation
protests, 25
  see also criticism, of U.S.-Iraq policies;

al Qaeda, 21, 23
Al-Quds Al-Arabi (newspaper), 37

Rautsi, Inari, 16–17
rebuilding, 56–57, 77
  see also cost, of rebuilding Iraq;
    problems; and specific areas of rebuilding
    effort
recession, 59–60
Red Cross, 44
religion, 63–64, 69, 73–75
  see also Islam; Muslims; Shias; Sunnis
Republican Guard, 27
resistance, to U.S. occupation
  allies of U.S. in Iraq affected by, 44–45
  characteristics of fighters in, 45–46
  constitution signing and, 76
  of foreign guerrilla fighters, 46–48
  humanitarian agencies affected by,
    42–43, 79

increase in troops and raids against, 48–50

Iraqis cooperating with U.S. affected by, 41–42

jihad and, 47–48

missile attacks on aircraft, 82

al Qaeda and, 46–48

Saddam Hussein and, 46

statistics about, 45

strategies of, 46

U.S. forces and administrators affected by, 39–41

Revolutionary Command Council, 16

Rice, Condoleezza, 34

Rumsfeld, Donald H., 14

sabotage. *See* resistance, to U.S. occupation

Saddam Fedayeen, 27

Sanchez, Ricardo, 47, 68

sanctions, 20–21

Sciolino, Elaine, 15

sects, 63–64

see also Islam; Muslims; Shias; Sunnis

self-rule, 64

see also Iraqi Governing Council

September 11, 2001, 21–22

Shias

demand for democracy by, 70–72

history of, 63–64

IGC and, 66

Iran and, 17–18

leadership of, 74

terrorist attacks on, 41, 42

Shiism. *See* Shias

Shiites. *See* Shias

Simons, Geoff, 15

Sistani, Ali al-, 66, 68–69, 70–72, 73, 74

Spratt, John. M., Jr., 58

Sunnis

Baath Party and, 15

demands of, for new government, 72–73

history of, 63–64

IGC and, 66

al Qaeda and, 48

Saddam Hussein regime and, 15

Sunnism. *See* Sunnis

Talabani, Jalal, 66

telephone networks, 81–82

temporary government. *See* Iraqi Governing Council

terrorism. *See* resistance, to U.S. occupation

Tikriti, Abid Hamid Mahmoud al-, 37

Timmerman, Kenneth R., 18

trade credit system, 89

transitional government, 70

see also Iraqi Governing Council

transportation, 82

Turkomans, 67

unemployment, 89

United Nations (UN)

attack on office of, 42–43

economic sanctions by, 88

election experts from, 72

financial support for Iraq program and, 61–62

humanitarian aid efforts of, 21

inspections for weapons of mass destruction and, 20

lack of support by, for Iraq War, 11, 24

mandate of, for U.S. to rebuild Iraq, 53–54

military aid to U.S. in Iraq and, 56

Monitoring, Verification, and Inspection Commission (UNMOVIC), 24

oil-for-food program of, 21, 29, 30, 44

participation of in Iraq rebuilding, 61

Persian Gulf War and, 18–19, 20, 21

purpose of, 62

Resolution 1483 of, 53–54

Resolution 1511 of, 56

Security Council objections to Iraq War, 23

Special Commission on Iraq (UNSCOM), 20

World Food Program (WFP), 30

U.S. Agency for International Development (USAID), 79, 80

water, 81

weapons of mass destruction (WMD), 11–12, 19–20, 34–36

Wheelock, Tom, 79

women, Iraqi, 86

World Bank, 54, 56, 57

World Health Organization (WHO), 29, 30

Zarqawi, Abu Musad al-, 47

Ziad, Homayra, 30

★ Picture Credits ★

Cover Image: © Shepard Sherbell/
   CORBIS
© Ali Abbas/EPA/Landov, 71
© Lynsey Addario/CORBIS, 43
© AFP /Getty Images, 35, 46, 65, 68, 84, 87
© Peter Andrews/Reuters/Landov, 22
© William Coupon/CORBIS, 57
Diseño Communications, 12, 19, 60
© DoD photo by William Turenne, 40

© Kieran Doherty/Reuters/Landov, 78
© Getty Images, 16, 25
© Atef Hassan/Reuters/Landov, 14
© Reuters/CORBIS, 32, 54, 59
© Reuters/Landov, 80, 83
© Patrick Robert/CORBIS SYGMA, 51
© Ricki Rosen/CORBIS SABA, 73
© Goran Tomasevic/Reuters/Landov, 26,
   29, 47

☆ About the Author ☆

Debra A. Miller is a writer and lawyer with an interest in current events and history. She began her law career in Washington, D.C., where she worked on legislative, policy, and legal matters in government, public interest, and private law firm positions. She now lives with her husband in Encinitas, California. She has written and edited numerous publications for legal publishers as well as books and anthologies on historical and political topics.